From the Unreached
Let Perception Radiate

Dall'irraggiunto irraggi percezione

From the unreached let perception radiate

Poems by Domingo Notaro

Foreword by Enrica Maria Ferrara

Translated from the Italian by Kay McCarthy

 **DALKEY ARCHIVE PRESS**

Library of Congress Cataloging-in-Publication Data
Names: Notaro, Domingo, 1939- author. | Ferrara, Enrica, 1969- writer of
foreword. | McCarthy, Kay (Catherine), translator. | Notaro, Domingo,
1939- Poems. Selections | Notaro, Domingo, 1939- Poems. Selections. English
Title: Dall'irraggiunto irraggi percezione = From the unreached let
perception radiate : poems / by Domingo Notaro ; foreword by Enrica Maria
Ferrara ; translated from the Italian by Kay McCarthy.
Other titles: From the unreached let perception radiate
Description: First Dalkey Archive editiion. | Victoria, TX : Dalkey Archive
Press, 2016. | A bilingual text in English and Italian.
Identifiers: LCCN 2016030602 | ISBN 9781628971781 (pbk. : alk. paper)
Subjects: LCSH: Notaro, Domingo, 1939---Translations into English. |
Experimental poetry, Italian.
Classification: LCC PQ4914.O83 .A2 2016 | DDC 851/.92--dc23
LC record available at https://lccn.loc.gov/2016030602

www.dalkeyarchive.com
Victoria, TX / McLean, IL / Dublin

Dalkey Archive Press publications are, in part, made possible through the support of
the University of Houston-Victoria and its programs in creative writing, publishing,
and translation.

Printed on permanent/durable acid-free paper

Foreword

Domingo Notaro's poetry is a miracle; not only in the sense that his verses force the reader to take a pause for reflection and stare in amazement at the geometrical web of intricate lyrical embroidery laid out onto the blank page, but also in a more literal and subjective sense. For Domingo Notaro himself is contemplating the wondrous birth of his poetry with the same candid simplicity that drove him to the arts in his early childhood, when he went out into the dark night and sketched images of light in the clear air with burning embers. Those images dissolved immediately afterwards, like fireworks or shooting stars, but their memory persisted in the poet's mind and caused the artist to hesitate in awe before the mystery of their creation. That trail of light which suddenly vanished acquired mythical status for the child, leading to the discovery of the elusiveness of all meaning which is captured in a fleeting moment through the eyes of the poet-child.

Later in life, Notaro will describe the creative process with words that keep a luminous trace of that archetypical moment in which the artist discovered his ability to challenge the dark womb of nature through the burning power of signifying embers:

> In creating the un-natural, metamorphosis occurs amid
> amazement and wild bewilderment only to find the self
> beyond the horizon of the present harbinger of our meager
> knowledge and awareness itself.
> The opus of fiery unknown revealing configuration
> Art—Poetry in the moonless night is the constellating arse-end
> of the firefly facing towards the other

*Nel creare l'innaturale metamorfosi avviene tra stupore e sgomento
    perdendosi per trovarsi*
*oltre l'orizzonte del presente precorrendo il nostro esiguo sapere e la
    stessa coscienza*
L'Opera d'ignito ignoto svelante configurazione
*L'Arte cioè la Poesia nell'illune notte è il culo costellante della luc-
    ciola all'altra protesa*[1]

Through these verses, written at the onset of the new millen-
nium, we are led back to that first dark night of Notaro's childhood
when the poet began to work on the "opus of fiery unknown reveal-
ing configuration" in which art and poetry live together and regener-
ate each other in symbiotic enmeshment. The reference to that first
symbolic moment in which the child sketched the night air with
his burning embers is more explicitly referred to if we consider the
original Italian verses: "*L'Opera d'ignito ignoto.*" Here, the mysterious
"unknown" [*ignoto*] turns into a figurative representation through
the aid of fire or flames, as the adjective "*ignito*" [fiery] suggests,
while the intermittence of light, which soon vanishes in the "moon-
less night," is irreverently alluded to through the juxtaposition of the
fireflies' posteriors stretched towards one another.

This is to say that poetry and figurative arts—if that is how we
should interpret the first term of the already mentioned pairing "Art-
Poetry"—march hand in hand, both sustaining Notaro to shape the
darkness of the world into a meaningful "configuration."

The symbolism described so far returns in one of the most sub-
stantial poems of the present collection, no. 44, *L'Art-E'* / "Art IS,"
that may be read as an ideal manifesto of Domingo Notaro's poet-
ics. In this poem, the artist is catapulted into a cosmic dimension,
becoming an astronaut who explores the depth of a starry universe,
trying to capture the immediacy of knowledge in the "rising" [*sor-
genza*] of a "vision" [*visione*].

there is no
                    evolution

1. *Domingo Notaro al complesso del Vittoriano. Oltre l'orizzonte, 2-27 maggio
2001*, with a preface by Carlo Bo (Rome: Eldec, 2001), 56–57.

but
ulterior
rising
the idea posterior
to vision
and no concept
can
replace deed
beacon
Memory of the Future
non c'è
evoluzione
ma
ulteriore
sorgenza
posterior l'idea
alla visione
e nessun concetto
può
sostituire il fare
faro
Memoria del Futuro

It is remarkable that the artist's intuition precedes his conceptual thinking. It is his *doing*, in fact, that performs the creation of knowledge by way of internalizing time and space so that memory is not representation of a mythical past but rather osmosis of past, present and future in the cathartic instant of his artistic performance. Far from suggesting a Pan-like identification of the poet with nature, Notaro's aesthetic seems to point in the direction of a post-human embrace between the artist-creator and the cosmos,[2] where the poet

2. This line of interpretation is confirmed by Notaro's engagement with cosmology, especially in the series of paintings entitled "Pluridimension" where, as noted by Guaraldo, "the scientist Notaro represents a 'Pluriverse' – a multiple universe – Einsteinianly bent, immersed in the cold light of the primordial big bang from which man is not excluded, but is no longer at the centre of the system, beginning and end of all" (C. Guaraldo, "Art and Science in the Work of Notaro," in *Domingo Notaro al complesso del Vittoriano*, cit., 15).

does not need to reproduce or represent energy or matter as something separate from him because he *is*, in fact, that very energy and that very matter:

> invisible
> blissfully
>> from the energy of matter
>>> to the matter
>> of energy
>>> arise
>>> the urge is

> style

> *in*
>> *visibilio*
>>> *dall'energia della materia*
>>>> *alla materia*
>>> *dell'energia*
>>>> *assurge*
>>>> *urge*
>>>>> *è*

> *lo stile*

Reading these verses, we can therefore assume that "style" or "form" is not something external and rational which has been superimposed or juxtaposed to a pre-existing "content." It can be argued, instead, that "style" is also an aggregation of matter and energy which has "arisen" with the same urgency which first occurred during the poet's "vision." Given the strong interest in physics and quantum physics displayed by Notaro on several occasions, and particularly in his figurative output, I believe that I am not pushing the boundaries of my interpretation too far if I attempt to read his poetry in the framework of Barad's performative or "agential realism." Grounded in the concept that reality is not an object of knowledge that is external to the cognitive subject but rather a "doing" or "becoming" in which subject and object are radically enmeshed and entangled with one another, performative realism may provide the perfect epistemological framework to understand Notaro's poetics. Based on this perspective, which may or may not be known to the artist but is grounded on the philosophical premises of quantum physicist Niels Bohr, "things do not have inherently determinate boundaries or properties, and words do not have inherently determinate meanings."[3] Instead, meaning and knowledge are *performed* during the "intra-action"[4] between subject and object, that is, the creator and his object of creation. In this context, we can better apprehend the image of the artist in voluntary exile from his contemporaries, with "a stampede of stars in the veins / the / mind / sinking / the concave into convex / lightning-quick" [*un calpestio di stelle nelle vene / la / mente / inabissando / il concavo in convessa / fulmineo*]; an artist who is able to perceive every "grain" and "throb" of the universe because nothing, no matter, is external to him. He becomes an object among other objects.

The question that one may reasonably be expected to ask is: what effect does this creative process have on the reader? Is the reader a necessary element in the production of creative signification? What role does he or she play in the intra-action between the poet's words and his world?

On first encountering Notaro's texts, one might infer that his readers are expected to formulate their own specific response to the artist's polysemous clusters of poetic matter scattered onto the page, which seem to condense the essence of the above-mentioned intra-action between subject and object. Of course, any readers of poetry— or readers *tout court*—are in fact called upon to express their own emotional, rational, intellectual response to a given text, a response which is largely conditioned by an array of cultural, historical, personal and social factors that will lead them to a re-symbolization of the text's intrinsic meaning, if such a beast actually exists.

In the case of Notaro's poetry, however, one cannot help but feel that the reader is caught in a sort of *mise en abyme* of the aesthetic process, in which the lyrical world designed onto the page

3. K. Barad, "Posthumanist Performativity: Toward an Understanding of How Matter Comes to Matter," *Signs* 28.3 (2003), 813.
4. The term "intra-action" rather than "interaction" is used by Barad to describe the world of phenomena which is defined as "the ontological inseparability of agentially intra-acting components" (815).

strives to reproduce, also in a visual way, the poet's performance in his quest for knowledge. Akin to a stream of consciousness retracing the steps of his creative encounter or intra-action with matter and energy, Notaro's verses expect and demand the reader's active role in the process of signification. Notaro's frequent use of rhetorical figures and tropes such as the palindrome, as well as his constant dissection and deformation of words' signifiers for the purpose of creating new internal meanings ("ego loss continues / by-dropping multiplies lapilli / with hassle-hexyl-I" [*l'ego nella perdita perdura / ac-cadendo moltiplica lapilli / d'assillo l-esil-io*], (*Rito continua all'orizzonte* / "Rite peering at the horizon") aim at producing defamiliarization and displacement.

When faced with a familiar word that suddenly acquires new layers of meaning, which in turn may spark entirely new signification processes, the reader is forced to take a long pause in the otherwise rapid flux of poetic imagery accelerated by a lack of punctuation, and to consider the world in a brand-new perspective. In the above cited verses, the loss of centre experienced by an exiled subject is marked by the passage from the strong "ego" to the weak "I," whose process of debilitation and fragmentation is visualized through the falling lapilli of the middle verse leading to the "*esil-io*" [hexyl-I]. Here the poet deconstructs the word "*esilio*" into its two internal signifiers, "*esile*" [fragile, weak] and "*io*" [I], which encourages the reader to adjust his semiosis and re-symbolization of the poet's words.

The deconstruction of the word "*esil-io*," translated as "hexyl-I," also provides us with a tiny example of the incredible challenge that Notaro's poetry lays before a literary translator. Kay McCarthy's translation uses the word "hexyl," a saturated radical compound of hydrogen and carbon, associated with the word "I," therefore performing a new process of signification which represents her own act of re-symbolization based on the form of the signifier, and its sound, rather than that of the signified. In other words, when encountering the obstacle of an untranslatable word or compound, McCarthy seems to follow Roman Jakobson's guideline in treating "phonemic similarity" as "semantic relationship."[5]

5.   Roland Jakobson, "On Linguistic Aspects of Translation," in *The Translation Studies Reader*, ed. Lawrence Venuti (New York: Routledge, 2004), 118.

This choice inevitably leads to what could be perceived as a potential loss of the original sense that the author intended to convey. In Notaro's case, however, the artist's continuous encouragement to an open and performative cognitive approach might lead us to believe that McCarthy's translation constitutes the perfect "objective correlative" of Domingo Notaro's poetic world, insofar as she responds to the poet's stimulus by intra-acting with his words and performing new clusters of meaning which, in turn, will lead to brand-new processes of signification in another language.

Drawing upon J. L. Austin's concept of performativity—which considers certain linguistic acts as a "doing" or "acting" rather than a simple "saying"—and upon Derrida's notion of iterability or citationality—based on which language always incorporates the acts of "others"—performativity has recently emerged in the field of translation and translation studies as the conscious production of a new text in the target language which is different from the original source text and holds nearly unlimited potential for literary *action*: "A new linguistic production results, one infused with the otherness of its source [...] translation's ostentatious iterability reveals a quite uncanny potential for literary *action*, presenting a text from elsewhere to a new audience, while creating a new language that will, in some sense, belong to (and disrupt) them both."

Sometimes it takes only one word, internally deconstructed in different ways in Italian and English, to project the newly translated text into another realm of multi-layered semiosis. I am thinking, for example, of the poem *O di se ha* / "Odd is see if," where the sudden adjectivization of the title text in the English version—originally aiming to imitate the phonetic substance of the word *Odissea* ["Odyssey"] and simultaneously conserve the breakdown of words constructing a new meaning—ends up casting a thick shadow onto the idea of cosmic conscience triumphantly described in the Italian poem, a shadow of "oddness" and doubt which is in fact absent in the source text: "Odd is see if / life still / possesses a / sense [*O di se ha / la / vita / senso ancora*]."

As regards the main themes and topics explored by Domingo Notaro in his verses, since we are so fortunate as to be presented with a selection of his complete poetic work from the 1960s to the present, we are able to appreciate the evolution in the topics he chooses to take on and in his formal approach to them. Some recurrent motifs include the themes of exile, fertility, and creation, woman as source of inspiration and reproductive matrix of thinking and organic matter, the human body enmeshed with cosmos, the corruption of those in power. However, there is a definite change in tone and spirit when we consider the production of the Sixties and Seventies and compare it with that of the Eighties and Nineties.

In the first two decades, we witness the poet's contemplation of the newly rediscovered world of his childhood—the Italian land to which he returns in his early twenties after having emigrated to Argentina at the age of nine—observed with a dispassionate but affectionate gaze. Despite the sense of estrangement experienced by the poet, and voiced through the wonderful lyrics of poems such as *Il sole è un gallo esploso* / "The sun is a rooster erupted on" and "Palermiti," the reader is propelled into a visual experience that combines past and present memories, virtually sewn together by drawing lines which design shapes and trajectories linking time and space. In Palermiti, the poet's native village, where "the stalks no longer stitch the air / with vertical needlesful of milk" [*le spighe non cuciono più l'aria / con gugliate verticali di latte*], one can still immerse oneself in the warmth "of stories scored with honey and salt / leavening like loaves / on the parchment of dark kitchens [*di storie graffite con parole di miele e sale / che lievitano come pani / sulla pergamena delle cucine buie*]," and the poet may still experience a sense of belonging with respect to the country and the people from which he departed in voluntary exile. However, we are left under no illusion of an idyllic return but rather with a sense of ambivalence, in which the poet's Italian origins become like an original sin of which he cannot rid himself, even though he likes to think that his "feet are roots of air [*piedi sono radici d'aria*]." As Notaro suggests in *Il sole è un gallo esploso* / "The sun is a rooster erupted on," his sense of estrangement, which leads him to disown his surroundings, is tainted by his suspicion that the disquieting scene witnessed by him—symbolized by the "sharp spurs of eagle," the "beggars on river-edges awaiting," and the spiked "enemy"—is also partly his responsibility, as we can see from his final admission of guilt: "the / sun / is / a / rooster / erupted / on the / pomegranate / dawn / I / do not / recognize / myself / innocent [*il /sole / è / un / gallo / esploso / sul / melograno / dell'alba / Io / non / mi / riconosco / innocente*]."

Conversely, Notaro's poetry of the Eighties and Nineties seems to completely discard any consoling tones as the artist inhabits the condition of exile as a perpetual immanent dimension, while he becomes almost a fugitive from his own country due to the unrestrained corruption spreading in his motherland. Aptly opened by the poem *D'èsili esìli che questo tempo impone* / "Of exile exiles which these times impose," this section of the volume allows the readers to sink deeply into the rotting "inferno" of a social scene dominated by "the horde of harrowing horrors [*l'orda d'orchi dilaniando*]" which ensures that "unsurpassed the middle ages persist" [*invalicato medioevo permane*]. From the domestic confines of "Italietta," the virulent decay of our contemporary world quickly spreads to other countries and continents, oblivious of the damage it may cause, infectious and seductive like the onomatopoeic blabbering of an infant in its prelogic stage:

Bàbbaobabbabel
Babel
baobab
bàb
scattered like sperm
I have found them
in the genital baycove
(bàbbaobabbabel) [. . .]
beyond the ditch of doleful waters
point of primordial juncture between
Europe
Africa
America

Bàb-baobab-babele
babele
baobab
bàb
sparsi come sperma
l'ho trovati
nella baia-foce-genitale
(bàb-baobab-babele) [...]

oltre il fossato di dolenti acque
nel punto d'unione primordiale
D'Europa
Africa
America

(*Bàbbaobabbabel* / "Bàbbaobabbabel")

It is not by chance that here the references to Dante's *Commedia*, usually exploited to describe the common condition of exile which unites the contemporary poet with his predecessor, are more explicitly drawn from the dark gothic images of *Inferno*—as in the image of the "ditch of doleful waters," quoted above, which is reminiscent of the Stygian swamp at the borders of the fifth circle of Hell. Generally speaking, many of the apocalyptic scenarios that constitute the pitiful and horrendous stage in which the roaming soul of the poet has to perform his artistic duties, are described through a dark imagery largely borrowed from Dante's *Inferno*.

It is as if, at this point in time, between the Eighties and the Nineties, Pablo Picasso's prophetic words about Notaro's art in 1972, began to acquire an overwhelming meaning for the poet himself who keeps struggling to fix his innocent gaze on the world of his contemporaries, a world that appears more and more fraught with inhumanity, cruelty, political fraud and rapine.

"You are a child-I with many centuries over and above your human stature [*Tu sei un io bambino con molti più secoli sopra la tua statura umana*]": these were Picasso's words, which can be considered ominous if we pay attention to Notaro's ability to regenerate his art throughout the decades by revitalizing that pure child-like gaze through which he observes the cosmos every time as if it were his first.

Overburdened and nearly crushed by an infamous State that leads the individual to experience hopelessness and despair—as in the poem *Bast-ardi* / "Bast-a-rds," in which the lyrical I gives in to the use of obscene language and imagery to signify the full extent of the outrageous deceit and corruption in the public sphere—the poet finds his rescue from the darkness of the Nineties through the power of myth which helps to propel his art into the freedom of cosmos and the performative aesthetics of the new millennium.

The turning-point in this process of discovery is represented, in my opinion, by the poem *La scia l'ascia lascia* / "The camber cleaver carves," in which the metamorphic power of logos is demonstrated both at the level of signifiers—through the alliterative strength of nouns and verbs generated by one another—and of the semantic field which is first alluded to and then fully constructed through the poem's central metaphor: the tree of life that is scraped and carved by the hatchet until either it "falters," or "if it fails to fall it / is / the Archetype [*ma se non cade* / *è* / *l'Archetipo*]. Life and logos are returned to their original archetypical matrix by way of stretching the limits of living matter and poetic words to the verge of destruction or nonsense. Only by doing so, can the artist experience that pre-logic vision which is at the core of his post-human aesthetics, as described in the poem *L'Art-E'* / "Art IS," which belongs, in fact, to this new stage of Notaro's poetics.

In the long poems of the new millennium, in which the reader is forced to chase the trail left by the poet's hatchet in his quest for the archetypical essence of life—by following the constant zigzag and ladder-shaped design of the verses rolling onto one another—Notaro seems to pursue a meta-aesthetic and interdisciplinary line of questioning as he interrogates himself about the nature of art: painting, sculpture as well as the arts in general are central themes of his poems. In all its forms, art is visualized as vital osmosis between life and art ("*innesco* / *innesto* /*innatural* / *e* / *tra* / *vitArte*" [rain-bow-ful inciting / unnatural / implant / twixt / lifeArt], *Pittura Ruttil* / "Ruptile painting"), organic and inorganic matter, rational awareness and visionary urgency, overcoming spatial and temporal boundaries through the power of *doing*: "*T-erra* / *v-erro anch'io* / *poi* / *che d'amorfo* / *offro* / *senso* / *al* / *Fare*" [Err-th / bo-err I too / then of / amorphous / offer / sense to / Deed] (*Pittura Ruttil* / "Ruptile painting").

Throughout this process, Notaro's exploration of language is reminiscent of that carried out by other writers of the Twentieth century who felt the urge to submit their language to a game of internal segmentation, subdivision, disaggregation and re-composition for the purpose of enhancing the signifying strength of their concepts. I am thinking of Joyce's pastiche of neologisms, portmanteau words and multilingual morphemes in *Finnegans Wake* or of Gadda's parodic and irreverent, fiercely subjective and expressionistic new language which, according to one of his scholars, exploded in "shards of incandescent expressivity."[6]

This evocative definition of Gadda's experimental approach to style coincidentally leads us back to our initial image of the poet-child brandishing his signifying embers to fight the darkness of nature and its elusive meaning. Conscious of his "illiteracy" in many alphabets—as in the exquisite poem *Analfabeta d'innumeri alfabeti* / "Illiterate in countless alphabets"—Notaro escapes the geometry and prefabricated moulds of stylistic conventions, which he calls "affabulating architectures" [*affabulanti architetture*], to embark in his own creative opus in which he behaves like a bird that joins together distant points of space and time through his "morning-oscillating sparrow-twitter" [*mattin-o-scillante passerio*]. Thus, the poet's ability to return such a plurilingual and pluristylist image of the world to his readers is linked to his particular talent to overcome the boundaries between himself and language, subject and object, art and matter, thanks to his oscillating and compacting gaze that behaves like a loom: "iris restoring / glow / is / day / loom-compacting thread / to / thread / so the bird may weave the sky / I live the azure living in his flight [*d'iride ridà / lucòre / è / giorno / telaio che compatta filo / a / filo / così l'uccello va tessendo il cielo / vivo l'azzurro vive nel suo volo*].

Indeed, halfway between lucid vision and prophetic hallucination, Notaro's poems seem to lean over the edge of an infinite vacuum—terrifying, at times, like the undifferentiated darkness of an Hegelian night, or overwhelmingly beautiful like the azure depth of a blue sky—a vacuum which the poet explores by virtue of his constant *doing*, through that child-like gaze identified by Picasso as the key element of his greatness:

> The artist's Doing
> is to be
>   Beacon Inducing to
>   See
>   whether every limitless seer-sign

---

6. In the original Italian text: *schegge di incandescente espressività* (Alberto Arbasino, "Genius Loci"), in *Certi romanzi* (Torino: Einaudi, 1977), 339–71.

Imitates

Il Fare dell'artista
faro inducente è

    al
    Vedere

        s-ogni segno il-limita

           non

          imita

(*Prelogica la Visione induce* / "Pre-logical, the Vision induces")

—ENRICA MARIA FERRARA

CONTENTS

CONTENTS

Dall'irraggiunto irraggi percezione

From the unreached let perception radiate

1. Due generazioni

a

mio

Padre

Più in là dei potenti la terra assorta
assorbe l'halitus d'amore proibito
la gioventù circùita util è

       il vento

sfregando affila lacrime gelate

         ariste

           aspre

suoni amari lassi

      solo una luce

         dai

           raggi

crepitanti scioglie dolci carezze

         che

           ignoravamo

sotto questo fuoco crepitano

        lugubremente

le frontiere che conosci

       come la fame

il triste dialogare

      dei fucili

        l'orizzonte

ossidato

    di sangue coagulato

         tumefatto

di pianto

    t'impiantarono

        un limite di fango che

tu nemmeno odiavi

      era colossale d'illune notte

Two generations

to

my

Father

Beyond the powerful the land engrossed
absorbs the halitus of prohibited love
circuited youth is useful

the chafing

wind sharpens icy tears

bitter

bristles

acrid weary sounds

only one light

from

the crackling

rays releases sweet caresses

that we

un-knew

beneath this fire crackle

lugubriously

the frontiers you know

like hunger

the sad exchange

of rifles

the horizon

oxidized

with congealed blood

swollen

with weeping

planted you

a limit of mire that

you did not even hate

colossal with moonless night

il muro
         strapparono
                i tuoi strumenti di barbiere
le casseruole di rame stagnato
                    esigui per
tante privazioni
            i castagni d'ostriche aculeate
aperte
        al frutto acceso
                di minuti concentrici

crateri
        onde il latte orlano sue perle oscure
tutte quelle piccole cose che comprendono
la quotidiana vita
            oggetti consunti
                    bruniti
dal tempo
         la cucina affumicata
                da geografia
e inverno
        il vino che fiumi
              accalca sulle labbra
traboccando atemporale spazio
                calcaree conchiglie
scoscese d'eretti noceti
            metamorfica mica che nutre
lo stupore
         il segreto che custodisce il legno
elementale filosofia dell'albero che elabora
l'essenza
        e molte altre cose s'aggrappolano
nel tuo quadrante intimo
            cinto alla mia memoria
anche se non nomino

the wall
           they snatched
                  your barber's trappings
the tin-coated copper casseroles
                        exiguous from
so many deprivations
                 the chestnut-trees' spiky-oysters
open
          to the burnished fruit
                        of minute concentric
craters
          where milk hems its dark pearls

all these tiny things that comprise
everyday life
             worn-out objects
                     browned
by time
             the kitchen smoke-stained
                     by geography
and winter
             the wine river-flowing
                   teeming the lips
overflow-filling a-temporal space
                calcareous shells
slopes of upright walnut groves
               metamorphic mica nourishing
astonishment
              the secret wood safeguard-conceals
basic philosophy of the tree elaborating on
the essence
            and many other things bunch
into your intimate quadrant
             strapped to my memory
though I do not name

Padre
     la rivoluzione non è una maschera
                      senza
palpebre
      ma un figlio che ama
               con la forza
delle tue radici
        per far scaturire le sue ali
nella mia gola
      un solco di carbone lasciò
                 scia
indelebile
      sciame di caustica tessitura
pugnali
     di sostanze penetranti
            stami ostili salgono
dai pantani
     solo a coprire di cicatrici
             le spighe
le viti nude che vacillano ansimando
            turpi
mentre svaniscono i cammini
         attraversati da
un freddo d'acciaio acuto
      ripugnante

Quando l' occàso si cancellò di nomi
            gocce
gote triste rosso
     ritornaro-no dal tedio
             gli
esseri feriti
    tra gli allori
      loro lacrime

Father
            revolution is not a mask
                                    devoid of
eyelids
            but a son who loves
                                    with the strength
of your roots
                to unshackle his wings
in my throat
                a ridge of carbon left
                                    indelible
wake
                swarm of caustic weave
daggers
                of penetrating substances
                                    hostile stamina rising
from the swamps
                only to cover with scars
                                    the shoots
of naked vines stumbling panting
                                    foully
while pathways vanish
                            crossed by
cold sharp steel
                            repugnant

When sundown was cancelled by names
                                    drops
sad red cheek
                                    the
injured beings
                un-returned from tedium
                    amid laurels
                                    their tears

volatili di miseria

          sconosciuti

               anteci

                    laceri

anhelanti di pace

          dai bambini pendevano

                        teneri

canti strangolati

        e

        NOI

          figli

             per non temere

la paura

      amalgamammo tutto

             UNENDOCI

                  Buenos Aires 1961
                  partendo per Itaca

volatile with indigence
            unknown
                    lacerated
                            forebears
desirous of peace
            from children swung
                            tender
strangled tunes
            and
                WE
                    children
                            so as not to dread
fear
            amalgamated all by
                    UNITING

                                    Buenos Aires 1961
                                    on leaving for Ithaca

2. Un bambino disegna per terra

(LA MISERIA)

Un bambino disegna per terra
un grande pane
tanto che pensa già
di aver mangiato
ai bimbi bisogna regalare
sempre cose utili

A child draws on the ground

(WANT)

A child draws a big loaf
on the ground
so large he thinks he's
already eaten
we must always give children
useful things

3. Avvinghiati nell'aria ferma

Avvinghiati nell'aria ferma
alle navi rinnovano asettico grigio
prima di salpare
nella città del porto c'è baldoria
luce soffusa
chitarre
puttane
marinai
tanta birra
whisky
residue carezze

Gli astemi in lussuosissimi stagni
mercanteggiano la guerra
in nome della pace
all'alba i cigni disperati delle onde
saranno decapitati
dagli squali d'acciaio

Clasped in the still air

Clasped in the still air
to the ships they renew aseptic gray
before sailing
in the harbor city high jinks
soft light
guitars
whores
sailors
loads of beer
whiskey
lingering caresses

The abstemious in superluxurious stagnant holds
trade in war
in the name of peace
at dawn wave-desperate swans
will be beheaded
by steel sharks

4. Se i campi di grano sapessero

Se i campi di grano sapessero che la mia anima alita
nelle sue spighe
per non tingersi di zolfo
e svanire definitivamente in cascate di catrame
se comprendesse il cammino
il significato dell'ultimo passo dove iniziare
senza tempo pietrificato in specchi di sabbia
se il gallo della menzogna non cantasse
tre volte prima di ogni nascimento
la rosa sarebbe un mazzo di chiavi
e la verità meno astratta del prezzemolo

If the cornfields knew

If the cornfields knew
my soul breathes
in their stalks
to avoid being sulfur-tinged
and vanish definitively in cascades of tar
if the pathway grasped
the meaning of that last step where
timeless petrified sand-mirrors begin
if the cock did not sing of lies
three times before each birth
the rose would be a bunch of keys
and the truth less abstract than parsley

5. I bambini e le bandiere

I bambini e le bandiere
non possono stare insieme
crescere senza limiti
crescere crescere
crescere
la morte è già una bandiera
ancora
i bambini debbono sapere
giocare per sapere
giocare giocare
giocare
come posta la vita
giocarsi
per non smarrirla
senza conoscerla
rincorrendo bandiere
più sporche di sangue che lenzuola da parto

Children and flags

Children and flags
cannot live together
to grow without limits
grow grow
grow
death is already a flag
yet
children need to learn
to play so as to know
play play
play
life the prize
to dare-risk
not to lose it
without knowing it
chasing flags
more blood-stained
than birth-bed sheets

6. Il sole è un gallo esploso

Il sole è un gallo esploso
sul melograno dell'alba

non mi riconosco
nel palpitante profilo delle colombe
o negli aguzzi spiedi delle aquile

non mi riconosco
nei mendicanti che ai margini dei fiumi aspettano
l'elemosina dalla vita o il nemico trafitto

non mi riconosco
nel lento flauto del giorno che striscia come un serpente
nell'arcaica preghiera che tinge il tramonto
nella sera tarlata di stelle ancora lontane
nella notte buia preservativa di pace mancata
il
sole
è
un
gallo
esploso
sul
melograno
dell'alba
Io
non
mi
riconosco
innocente

The sun is a rooster erupted on

The sun is a rooster erupted on
the pomegranate dawn

I do not recognize myself
in the pulsating profile of doves
or in the sharp spurs of eagles

I do not recognize myself
in beggars on river-edges awaiting
life's alms or the enemy spiked

I do not recognize myself
in the slow flute of day sliding
snake-like
in the archaic prayer-tinged sunset
in the worm-eaten evening of stars still remote
in the peace-wanting protective dark night
the
sun
is
a
rooster
erupted
on the
pomegranate
dawn
I
do not
recognize
myself
innocent

7. Ho cercato un pezzo di carta

Ho cercato un pezzo di carta
per intrappolare un'idea
ho messo il bianco della carta
verso l'alto
l'azzurro della penna sulla carta
il tutto poggiato su qualcosa
che nascendo
metterà nuovamente
tutto in discussione

I sought a piece of paper

I sought a piece of paper
to trap an idea
I faced the paper-white
upward
the pen-blue on the paper
all resting on something
that upon birth
will question
everything once more

8. La casa andava a spasso

La casa andava a spasso
con tutti i suoi balconi
nell'ombra silenziosa
che il sole raccontava prima di coricarsi
eppure
le bandiere
non amano la mia indipendenza
gli stendardi non chiedevano
che essere intoccabili
i tabù possedevano preghiere e pistole
in questo ambiente crebbi
impastando la farina dei giorni
al lievito delle idee divenni panettiere
ma ancora
qualche volta
molto spesso accade
il mio pane è
amaro

The house went a-walking

The house went a-walking
balconies and all
in the silent shadow
the sun told before lying down to rest
and yet
the flags
do not like my independence
the banners asked only to
be untouchable
taboos possessed prayers and pistols
in this environment I grew up
kneading the flour of days
into the yeast of ideas I became a baker
and yet
at times
very often
it happens
that
my
bread
is
bitter

9. Non sono assente

Non sono assente
sono lontano
quasi dentro le cose che amo

I am not absent

I am not absent
I am far away
almost inside the things that I love

10. Il cane non vide

Il cane non vide
mai manna dal cielo cadere
l'uomo
scrisse su tutti i suoi taccuini
che
il
cane
è il suo migliore amico
ma nonostante
lo batte ancora con il bastone
ed il cane immobile
sotto i colpi resta come prima
il
cane
che gli dà sicurezza
dunque (se mai)
essere padrone dell'amico
non
è
da
cani

The dog never saw

The dog never saw
manna fall from the sky
man
wrote in all his jotters
that
the
dog
is his best friend
and yet
he still beats him with a stick and the dog motionless
beneath the blows remains as before
the
dog
that makes him feel safe
so (if at all)
being the master of a friend
is
not a thing
for
dogs

11. Palermiti

Palermiti
nel Sud
dove sono nato
la turgida mammella del paese
contende la geografia alle ginestre
le lenzuola distese sull'erba
come fantasmi abbattuti nel sonno
ora le case crescono con l'assenza dell'uomo
sotto il cielo che si apre al giorno
ormai disabitato del suo profilo ricurvo all'orizzonte
muoiono le vigne nell'ossido delle sparizioni
e le spighe non cuciono più l'aria
con gugliate verticali di latte
Un piccolo paese (senza regali dimore)
nell'itinerario delle rondini
come una caverna rovesciata al sole
di storie graffite con parole di miele e sale
che lievitano come pani
sulla pergamena delle cucine buie
gli ulivi tanti arcieri vegetali
che hanno donato l urlo alle cicale
per rimanere gesto silenzioso
di mani tormentate che impugnano germinazioni
e d'emigranti soli per una beffa astrale
la gente torna vecchia
con il cuore ferito come un salvadanaio
sotto il vestito nuovo « made in »
per la farsa finale
e a vespri e caroselli si consola
Piccolo paese del Sud che mi hai visto nascere
i miei piedi sono radici d'aria
che sfiorano la terra

Palermiti

Palermiti
in the South
where I was born
the turgid breast of the hamlet
contends its geography with the gorse
sheets spread out on the grass
like ghosts felled in their sleep
now the houses grow with the absence of man
under a sky opening up to the day
now stripped of its bent profile on the horizon
the vineyards die in the rust of disappearances
and the stalks no longer stitch the air
with vertical needlesful of milk
A small hamlet (with no regal dwellings)
on the swallows' itinerary
like a cave upturned in the sun
of stories scored with honey and salt
leavening like loaves
on the parchment of dark kitchens
the olive trees so many herbal archers
donating cicadas their wail
to remain the silent deed
of tormented hands grasping germinations
and of solitary immigrants due to an astral jest
the people return old
their hearts sore like a moneybox
beneath a new suit "made in"
for the final farce
consoling themselves with vespers and carousels
Little village of the South which saw my birth
my feet are roots of air
that brush the earth

ma ormai sono lontano
non per aver attraversato fiumi
libri città dolori continenti
amori oceani nemici stagioni e sogni
ma perché non baratto le mie ali
di te mi è rimasto lo schiaffo della fame
ed i colori della luce nel sangue come navi
ma anche la tristezza di sentirti vuoto
dietro le facciate che fingono di crescere
con i trenta denari delle maschere che ritornano
per comprare il nulla che indossa la speranza
al prezzo della vita inutilmente truffata

but I am far away by now
not because I have crossed rivers
books cities hurts continents
loves oceans enemies seasons and dreams
but because I do not barter my wings
of you the whack of hunger has remained
and the colors of the light in blood like ships
but also that sadness on feeling empty
behind façades that fake growth
for the thirty coins of the masks returning
to buy hope-donning nought
at the cost of life misled in vain

12. Crebbi

Crebbi
come un albero
e persi le radici
per divenire uccello

I grew

I grew
like a tree
and shed my roots
to become a bird

13. Se fisso la sera con sguardo assente

Se fisso la sera con lo sguardo assente
e l'ombra accucciata ai miei piedi
impassibile resta
non domandarmi nulla
sono uscito a pascolare la mia animalità

If I stare blankly at the evening

If I stare blankly at the evening
and the shadow crouching at my feet
remains impassive
do not ask me anything
I have gone out to graze my
animality

14. L'uomo spese piedi e calzari

L'uomo spese piedi e calzari
per raggiungere il cielo
che all'orizzonte alla terra si univa
ma fu inutile
allora costruì una torre gigantesca
finché la sua lingua si confuse
e mastini inquisitori lo calunniarono
studiò gli uccelli per capire il volo
e ancora fu deriso e condannato
per superbia e presunzione
angelo o demone credi di essere
per tanto osare
ma l'uomo tacque e volò

Man wore out feet and footwear

Man wore out feet and footwear
to reach the sky
that on the horizon met the earth
but it was useless
so he built a gigantic tower
until he confused his tongue
and mastiff inquisitors slandered him
he studied birds to grasp flight
and again was mocked and sentenced
for pride and presumption
angel or demon you think you are
for daring so much
but man fell silent and took flight

15. Madre mia (a John lettera non scritta)

Madre mia:
una sola specie di uomini ora conosco
ma sono troppo morto per poterlo dimostrare
mentre sul fosso fioccano le rondini
verde sale l'erba cresciuta nel bruciato
la mia faccia copre la terra
con la fronte grandinata
il sipario delle palpebre è calato
le mie mani come pesci all'amo
ancora mordono il fucile
freddo a freddo
a inverno tramontato oltre l'acqua salata
tu aspetterai invano il mio ritorno
ma non accettare il mio nome
(in nero graffiato in marmo bianco)
d'inutile eroe lontano dalla vita
mentre
sul fosso fioccano le rondini
madre mia
una sola specie d'uomini ora conosco

P. S.
proprio adesso non vorrei essere così morto
portato come esempio
perché tutto ciò non si capisca

Mother dear (to John an unwritten letter)

Mother dear:
I know only one kind of man now
but I'm too dead to be able to prove it
while over the ditch swallows flock
green grown grass rises through the burn
my face covers the earth
the forehead riddled
the curtain of the eyelids lowered
my hands like fishes on hooks
still clench the rifle
cold by cold
at winter's sunset over the salt water
you will await my return in vain
but do not accept my name
(black scratched on white marble)
a useless hero far from life
while
over the ditch swallows flock
Mother dear
I know only one kind of man now

P.S.
right now I would I were not so dead
borne as an example
so that all this may not be understood

16. NO (a Ivan testimonianza non pervenuta)

NO
NO No
no no no
si si si
sI SI
SIberia
E PUR SI MUOVE

NO (to Ivan undelivered testimony)

NO
NO NO
no no no
yes yes yes
yEs YES - SS I
SIberia
AND YET IT MOVES

17. È mattino

È mattino
oggi 8 Aprile
quando
ancora
la tenerezza apre le ali del verde
tu
gli
occhi
ma non spegni il fuoco d'amore
dopo la ripida ascesa
come il salmone ritorni all'antica dimora
celebre-Picasso-grande-Pablo-eppure incompreso

È primavera a Mougins
ancora
una
volta
falchi mercenari ti porteranno al fosso
magari in spalla
indosseranno ombre funebri le loro facce
ed
io
incomincio a capire
Amico
Pablo
Genio
Picasso
perché la storia si ripete

It is morning

It is morning
today the eighth of April
when
again
tenderness opens the wings of greenness
you
your
eyes
but you don't quench the fire of love
after the steep climb
like the salmon you return to your ancient dwelling
famous-great-Pablo-Picasso-and yet misunderstood

It is spring in Mougins
one
more
time
mercenary hawks will carry you to the grave
on their shoulders perhaps
their faces wearing funerary shadows
and
I
begin to understand
Friend
Pablo
Genius
Picasso
why history repeats itself

18. **Avevo in mente un ritratto** *(a Pablo Neruda)*

Avevo in mente un ritratto
da farti
in rosso e azzurro
all'ora in cui nasce il giorno
o la notte
L'estate più levigata
avrei voluto
o l'autunno
pregno di frutti il pennello
per popolare la terra della tua carne
ed i tuoi occhi di fiume abitare
e al posto del cuore uccelli
voli per vene
o ruscelli
albe
alberi nelle tue mani piantare

Avevo in mente un ritratto
da partorire a dicembre
quando i cristalli del freddo traspaiono
e l'alito ha colore di metallo
ma
è la più triste primavera del Cile
le viscide tarme mercenarie
i servi felloni
i torturatori
i frigidi depravati
senza orgasmi d'amore
ad un Uomo hanno imposto la morte
per opprimere un Popolo
ancora i parassiti corazzati
le cimici del fascismo

I had in mind a portrait *(to Pablo Neruda)*

in red and sky-blue
in the hour when day is born
or night
I would have liked
the smoothest summer
or autumn
my brush full of fruit
to people the earth with your flesh
your eyes with river
and instead of a heart birds
flights for veins
or streams
sunrises
plant trees in your hands

I had in mind a portrait
to give birth to in December
when crystals of cold appear
and breath has the color of metal
but
it is Chile's saddest spring
the slimy mercenary moths
felonious servants
torturers
frigid depraved
devoid of love's orgasms
imposed death upon a Man
to oppress a People
still the armored parasites
the lice of fascism

e a te l'amara cicuta
poeta che non hai taciuto

Avevo in mente un ritratto
ma
è nato un grido
ch'è pugno
pugnale
penna per valicare
il silenzio o la menzogna
dei complici
e dei predoni

and bitter hemlock to you
poet who did not remain silent

I had in mind a portrait
but
a cry was born
which is a fist
dagger
pen to surpass
the silence or the falsehood
of accomplices
and predators

19. Ho finito il cielo

*"Non è possible bagnarsi due volte
nello stesso fiume"*
Eraclito di Efeso – V sec. a. C.

Ho finito il cielo
sgomitolando i miei battiti
solo
come un faro nelle trame della notte
e i capelli d'acqua in una cariatide di pioggia
ho
finito
ho finito il silenzio di tante parole
le porte da bussare
la geografia
e il nome dei giorni
le provocazioni
i sogni
le speranze
un percorso
ho
finito
fino a schiudermi
sgranando ogni grano dalla melograna della mia tristezza
e offrirvi questo pane d'amore
colmo calice di tentazioni che vi appartiene
quando ancora vivere è un'utopia
immorale il suicidio
ho finito la follia
che nelle ossa il vento mi ha inciso
ed i fantasmi che sbucciano logore confessioni
alle finzioni della realtà
chi mercanteggia ho finito
scorza di scarsa polpa

I have finished the sky

*"You cannot bathe twice
in the same river"*
Heraclitus of Ephesus – V cent. B.C.

I have finished the sky
unspooling my strokes
alone
like a beacon in the weave of night
and hair of water in a caryatid of rain
I have
finished
I have finished the silence of many words
the doors to knock upon
geography
and the name of the days
the provocations
dreams
hopes
a pathway
I have
finished
to the point of disclosing myself
plucking every pip from the pomegranate of my sadness
and offering you this bread of love
chalice full of temptations belonging to you
when to live is still utopia
suicide immoral
I have finished madness
that the wind has etched into my bones
and the ghosts that skin worn-out confessions
the fiction of reality
I have finished those who haggle
pulp-impoverished peel

negli incorruttibili corrotti cantieri d'idoli
per strategia potrei mettere in bocca
ad altri ciò che penso
ma il mio destino oramai
non è lo stesso destino
già non m'appartiene ciò che sono stato
l'impronta staccata da me
non è più mia
un volo
nella caduta che ascende dalla vita alla morte
ho finito i tranvai
che cuciono alla città la tenda del cielo
le mele cotogne ho finito
quando smessa la peluria del verde
accumulano carati
per raggiungere l'oro della maturazione
ma il più delle volte imputridiscono
smarrite nell'acerbo pallone delle insidie
tronchi cavi abitati dal letargo dei ghiri
e dalla copula degl'insetti
ho finito
rossa l'argilla plasmata
dall'esorbitante sorba dell'esilio
e le chiavi siderali del poeta
che in me sua lingua vive
e un fuoco l'alimenta e penetra
moltiplicando il canto
le finestre ho finito
uteri sull'orlo azzurrato del quarzo
dove incestuoso nomade m'affaccio
ho
finito
i
miracoli
dei tasselli neri delle notti

in the incorruptible corrupt building yards of idols
for strategy I might put into the mouths
of others what I think
but my destiny now
is not the same destiny
already what I have been belongs to me no more
the imprint torn from me
is no longer mine
a flight
in the fall that ascends from life to death
I have finished the tramcars
I have finished the quinces that
having shed the fuzz of green
accumulate carats
to reach the gold of maturation
but most of the time they rot
in the bitter ball of pitfalls
hollow trunks inhabited by hibernating dormice
and the copulation of insects

I have finished
red clay molded
by the exorbitant rowan of exile
and the sidereal keys of the poet
whose language lives in me
fed and penetrated by fire
multiplying song
I have finished windows
wombs on the azure edge of quartz
where incestuous nomad I gaze
I have
finished
the
miracles
of the blacks dowels of nights

intarsiati ai bianchi tasselli dei giorni
dove la posta in giuoco è la vita
del presente ho finito lo specchio
di tanto futuro e passato
trentatre anni ho finito
di tanto mutare
per
ancora
ancora rinascere

inlaid with the white tiles of the day
where what is at stake is life
i have finished the mirror
of so much future and past
thirty-three years have i finished
of so much change
yet
again
to be
reborn

20. Le parole cadono trascinando pensieri

Le parole cadono trascinando pensieri
come macchie che assumono forme mai definitive
le stagioni del linguaggio si susseguono
ardono e muoiono
nascono da incontenibili desideri
le parole cadono trascinando pensieri
oggi l'amore ha il tuo volto
nei tuoi occhi in fioritura si espandono le galassie
ed io l'astronomo che senza comprendere
osserva stregato
le parole cadono trascinando pensieri
la realtà che si mostra senza rivelarsi mai
il grano dei nostri corpi
versato in un mare di papaveri
dove i battiti delle tue ali passano
e il calice delle parole
piccioni impauriti rimangono segrete
quante cifre cadranno dai rami della notte
con i sorrisi spenti di fiori già appassiti
all'ombra travolgente di tutto ciò che passa
il vento scioglierà semafori e cavalli
ma tu ricorderai questi magici incontri
ed io senza ricordo avrò di te una lucciola
per l'abbecedario della mia tristezza
e per la solitudine un giocattolo
le ore rimarranno pesci imprigionati nelle reti degli
                                        orologi
gli uccelli migratori delle tue carezze
ritorneranno libere sull'isola del mio corpo
e troveranno ancora le biciclette del silenzio gareggiare
inseguendo il piccolo scolare dell'ignoto
che su fogli di specchio disegna utopie

Words fall hauling thoughts

Words fall hauling thoughts
like stains assuming never-fixed forms
the seasons of language follow on each another
burn and die
born of uncontainable desires
words fall hauling thoughts
today love has your face
in your eyes in bloom galaxies expand
and i the astronomer without comprehending
observe bewitched
words fall hauling thoughts
the reality which shows but never reveals itself
the seed of our bodies
poured out in a sea of poppies
where the beats of your wings pass
and the chalice of words
frightened pigeons remain secret
how many cyphers will fall from the branches of night
with the snuffed-out smiles of already-wilted flowers
in the overwhelming shade of all that passes
the wind will dissolve semaphores and horses
but you will remember these magical encounters
and I without recall will you as a firefly
for the spelling-book of my sadness
and the loneliness of a toy
the hours will remain fish imprisoned in the webs of
                                            timepieces

the migratory birds of your caresses
will return free to the isle of my body
and find once more the bicycles of silence racing
following that little scholar of the unknown
who upon sheets of mirror draws utopias

21. Donna

Donna
dal delta delle dita dei tuoi piedi
risalgo il fiume del tuo territorio
di madreperla e flauti minerali
raggiungo il planetario delle tue ginocchia
e scalo ancora
la carne della roccia e l'alito dei prati
alla pura dimora più tenera del muschio
ai roseti che ardono nel vulcano del canto
dallo spazio ai fianchi
ai semi dei tuoi capezzoli
gocce di giorno aperto da tutta la rugiada
al collo tuo che sale verticale e nudo
sfidando gigli e cereali
alla neve che si affaccia a grappoli
dal frutto aperto delle tue labbra
ai tuoi occhi dove tutto nasce
alle tue mani che creano carezze
alle conchiglie delle orecchie tue levigate a suoni
fino ai tuoi capelli d'antica vegetazione marina
Donna
ieri sei stata il continente sommerso dalle fecondazioni
oggi sei la compagna che di alba in alba
si conquista la storia
rinventando la libertà
che l'uomo aveva smarrito privandotene
nell'impero del profano e del sacro
dove il fuoco s'eclissa e marcisce la cenere
il serpente dell'ombra protegge i randelli
e le inferriate di chi cospira
i latrati corrosi dei sicari
dietro le torri del silenzio ghigliottinano i cigni

Woman

Woman
from the delta of your toes
I ascend the river of your land
of mother-of-pearl and mineral flutes
I reach the cosmos of your knees
and climb again
the flesh of the rock and the breath of the meadows
to the pure abode softer than moss
to the rose gardens that burn in the volcano of song
from space to your hips
to the seeds of your nipples
drops of day open to all dew
to your neck rising up vertical and naked
challenging lilies and corn
to the snow that appears in clusters
from the open fruit of your lips
to your eyes where everything is born
to your hands that create caresses
to the shells of your ears smoothened by sounds
as far as your hair of ancient marine vegetation
Woman
yesterday you were the continent submerged by fecundation
today you are the companion who from dawn to dawn
conquers history
reinventing freedom
that man had lost depriving you of it
in the empire of the profane and the sacred
where fire is eclipsed and rots the ash
the snake of the shadow protects the cudgels
and railings of those who conspire
the corroded barking of cut-throats
behind the towers of silence guillotine swans

e nelle fognature naviga la morte con dentiere e coltelli
le carceri aspettano con torture l'intelligenza
ragni senza sogni tessono vendette
nere larve mercenarie tarlano le sillabe
divorandone la crescita con il pretesto dell'ordine
dunque è arrivata l'ora
Donna
il giorno è un ciliegio
che ti aspetta per fiorire
ti aspetta l'aroma dei gabbiani appena nati
con voli e arcobaleno
e tu non più partorirai con dolore
ma veglierai con amore
il
Futuro

and in drains death sails with dentures and knives
prisons await intelligence with torture
dreamless spiders weave revenge
black mercenary larvae woodworm syllables
devouring growth under pretext of order
so the time has come
Woman
the day is a cherry
awaiting you to bloom
the aroma of newborn seagulls awaits you
with flights and rainbow
and you shall no longer give birth in pain
but keep loving vigil over
the
Future

22. Ti amo in ogni donna

Ti amo in ogni donna
che attraversa le mie carezze
che matura i miei pensieri
ti vivo con la vita
che mi gioco con l'attimo
ogni attimo
dove il tuo volo di brezza marina
fa ondeggiare il mio cuore
con mareggiate di battiti
già sono stato nel tuo abbraccio totale
ancora prima di nascere
già sono stato l'abitante ribelle
della tua anima già sono stato
e sempre per amore emigro
mi espando come il tuo sguardo
mi sprigiono per liberarti
e incontrarti
e liberarmi
all'infinito

I love you in every woman

I love you in every woman
who crosses my caresses
who ripens my thoughts
I live you with life
which I wager in a moment
every moment
where your marine-breeze flight
sways my heart
with flood-tides of beats
I have been in your total embrace
already before birth
I have already been the rebel dweller
of your soul I have already been
and for love I shall emigrate
I dilate like your gaze
I unleash myself to free you
and meet you
and free
to infinity

23. Ormai le scimmie dipingono

Ormai le scimmie dipingono
come bambini
i bambini pensano come adulti
gli adulti fanno stazioni orbitanti
come iddio
e
gli
uomni

Nowadays even monkeys paint

Nowadays monkeys paint
like children
children think like adults
adults make orbiting stations
like god
and
men

24. Sei come una terra antica

Sei come una terra antica
da dove i tunnel dei tuoi occhi arrivano
per un attimo felice

Sei il ruscello che abita il mio prato
all'ora in cui il verde pulsa
e i passeri si inseguono per disegnare l'aria

You are like an antique land

You are like an antique land
from which the tunnels of your eyes arrive
for an instant happy

You are the brook dwelling in my meadow
at the hour when the green throbs
and sparrows play chase to trace
the air

25. Vegliare negli occhi tuoi

Vegliare negli occhi tuoi
percorrerti
navigarti
con tutti i voli abitarti
nascere
nelle
tue
mani

Keeping vigil within your eyes

Keeping vigil within your eyes
browsing you
navigating you
with all those flights dwell in you to
be born
in
your
hands

26. D'èsili esili

D'èsili esìli che questo tempo impone
a chi randagio per non abiurare vive
penelopeo di segreto uccello vi riscopro
la meridiana che mia mente induce
da ovunque a Sud

Macero il mio fogliame humus diviene
felce equiseto ulivo vite melograno
fico ciliegio noce pesco bianco
cachi acquisito
castagno quercia pino del mediterraneo
tale la partenza quale l'arrivo

D'ossa osa il mio midollo le vestigia
che d'ogni oblio ritornano clamando
cos'è che rende inospitale luogo
ove l'ingegno brillò cotanto umano
d'illuminare la storia e poi svanire
immemore depresso nel degrado
nell'assenza dei figli prodighi o prodigi
api che d'alvo favo paria sono
ad altri alveari van donando miele
volto il volto verso meridione

Solare taumaturgico trauma
sonar mai sopito che onde emana
dai remoti racconti tramandati da voce d'avi
(l'orda d'orchi dilaniando dilagò
e invalicato medioevo permane)
allo spettro della favola fatale dell'esistere
che annega nello specchio pur permanendo
d'erranti erranti identità illusoria

Of exile exiles

Of exile exiles which these times impose
on the vagrant who to avoid abjuring lives
Penelopead of secret bird where I rediscover
the meridian that draws my mind
from everyplace southwards

I macerate my foliage the humus becomes
fern equisetum olive vine pomegranate
fig cherry walnut white peach
acquired persimmon
chestnut oak Mediterranean pine
departure exactly like arrival

The marrow of my bone dares to don the garb which
from all oblivion returning proclaims
what makes inhospitable the place
where such humane genius shone
illuminating history only to vanish
unmindful depressed into degradation
in the absence of prodigal or prodigious offspring
bees driven from the homehive's comb to
alien hives to hoard their honey
I face my face southwards

Solar thaumaturgic trauma
unplaced sonar weaving waves
of far-off fables flowing from ancestral voices
(the horde of harrowing horrors hove
while unsurpassed the middle ages persist)
to the phantom of the fatal fable of existence
drowning in the mirror yet enduring
in misplaced meandering illusionary identity

di novelle novelle per futura progenie
eppure cuore non solo di mareggiate
ogni dove m'errabondi
ma quasar oltre m'induci

Chi bandisce ancora l'allegria temendo
che gioia aspre rughe col ridere cancelli
e con esso rotto l'incantesimo arcano
tanatofobia sparisca liberando
da servile ombra arrogante ed avara
che vanifica ogni alba il nuovo giorno
regredendo lo stame della vita
nell'estremo stabbio ad indole indolente

Vile-o-vile che avvilisci l'umano
perché turba non turbi
non basta la fatica che tarpi gli arti
ma ai leali
le ali perennemente recidere bisogna

Grani cadendo in ogni dove dalla spiga
l'unica certezza il male originale
a dismisura patendo d'oppio l'oblio
perché lo sguardo oltre occhio nulla veda
e disseminati si perdano imputridendo
nelle viscere dei predoni che nutrono grami
o si trovano nel mistero semi in gestazione
gesto gesta Gesta
messi nelle messi ovunque per non abdicare

Ogni ricordo scorda la migrante fronda
nella deriva che dirada o addensa
accadimento perenne il de-perire
ma dal macero magico sostanza ridona all'albero
con-geniale galattica gemmazione

of novel novellas for future progenies
yet not the heart of sea-storms alone
wherever I roam enticing
me beyond quasars

Some still banish mirth lest
joy with laughter smooth the bitter lines
and with the arcane enchantment broken thus
thanatophobia vanish freeing
from enslaving arrogant avid shadow
that thwarts each new day at dawn
reducing the stamen of life
to listless laziness in endmost enclosure

Foul offence offending humanity
to rouse the rabble
limblopping fatigue does not suffice
but the wings of the faithful
must be continually cut

Grains fall far from the wheatear
the sole certainty primeval evil
experiencing excess of anodyne oblivion
lest the vision view beyond the eye
and thus scattered the go astray arotting
in the guts of marauders they nourish grudgingly
or find in mystery seeds gestating
gesture gests Gesta
sown with the seed against abdication

Each mind unmindful of the migrant frond
drifting diluted or dense
decline perennial circumstance
but the magic macerated matter restores to the tree
congenial galactic gemmation

tenero virgulto dura nel ramo
d'onde legno s'accresce dal midollo all'alburno
gemica resina la corteccia aroma

Con disperanza voce anti-ca-nto
l'illimite
d'istante distante di fluidità impastato
d'epochè l'epos riverberante sveli
l'aureo magma fecondo
propiziando
che alba ventura comunque non si perda
dovunque il vero ritorno
è
la
memoria

tender shoot hard in the bough
from whence wood swells from pith to alburnum
gemmary resin perfumes the bark

With unhopeful voice I antiphon
the limitless
distant instant of fluidity kneaded
with the throbbing epos of ages revealing
fecund gilded magma
auguring
that the coming dawn may not be lost
wherever true return
is
memory

27. Bàb-baobab-babele

Bàb-baobab-babele
babele
baobab
bàb
sparsi come sperma
l'ho trovati
nella baia-foce-genitale
(bàb-baobab-babele)
ai margini oltre la membrana
della cittadella d'invisibili mura
oltre il fossato di dolenti acque
nel punto d'unione primordiale
D'Europa
Africa
America
dove (dopo i continenti alla deriva)
l'utero dell'Hudson si dilata
E l'Atlantico sbava la sua spuma
bàb-baobab-babele
l'ho trovati sparsi come sperma
le etnie istillate nelle membra
la pelle tutte le uve dell'autunno
flora marina plasmata nei capelli
d'ogni carnosità di frutto labbra
nei volti i cereali della terra
(babele-baobab-bàb)
geografie di galassie inesplose
nei
sorrisi
negli occhi inabissati
sibil-Ibis di nitore
come sperma sparsi l'ho trovati
oltre i dissimulati ponti levatoi

Babbaobabbabel

Babbaobabbabel
Babel
baobab
bab
scattered like sperm
I have found them
in the genital baycove
(bàbbaobabbabel)
on the margins beyond the membrane
of the invisiblewalled citadel
beyond the ditch of doleful waters
point of primordial juncture between
Europe
Africa
America
where (following continental drift)
the uterus of the Hudson dilates
And the Atlantic craves its spray
Bàbbaobabbabel
I have found them scattered like sperm
ethnos bred in their limbs
skin all of autumn grapes
marine flora forged in their hair
lips of every fruity fleshiness
in their faces the grains of the earth
(bàbbaobabbabel)
geographies of unexploded galaxies
in the
smiles
of hollow eyes
Sybil-Ibis of clarity
like scattered sperm I have found them

le arterie
i raccordi
e le usurate spire dei gironi
(bàb-baobab-babele)
della metropolitana-flebofogna
che all'alba adesca al miraggio
ingurgita
introietta
e poi
nevrotiche-fluttuanti-regredite
scorie
spurga
nel livido pantano della sera
dileguando diluvia
finché notte tutto accoglie nel suo grembo
d'epochè epocale
e rigenerati
ancora argillosi
li partorisce al giorno nuovo e uguale
allora
dal parto senza nascita
tornano
ai building-bulldog
(verticali-tiranno-cani che mordono il ciel)
per versare ancora una quota di miele
bàb-baobab-babele
l'ho trovati sparsi come sperma
identici irriconoscibili ancora
in un lavico levarsi aurorale
bàb-baobab-babele
babele miasmatica
che all'apocalittico terrore immola
baobab dei frutti feti indistinti
ad effimeri riti demenziali omologa
bàb stellare della consapevolezza

beyond dissimulated drawbridges
the arteries
the links
and the threadbare loops of the gyres
(bàbbaobabbabel)
of the subwaydripsewer
that at dawn ensnares with its mirage
guzzles
ingests
later to
throw up
neuroticfloatingregressed
waste
upon the livid evening swamp
dispelling downpours
until night welcomes all to its
epochal era bosom
and regenerated
still clayey
generates them in the new identical day
then
from labour without birth
they return
to bulldog- buildings
(verticaltyrantdogs bite the sky)
to go on pouring their quota of honey
bàbbaobabbabel
I have found them scattered like sperm
identical unrecognisable still
in lavic auroral reveille
bàbbaobabbabel
miasmic Babel
which to the apocalyptic terror immolates
baobabs of fruitful indistinct foetuses
with ephemeral demential rites homologous

aperta all'identità nuova
Manhattan angolare mandala
isola
crisalide archetipale dell'evo metamorfico
da dove uno e trino
(oltre l'arrogante balbuzie)
l'uomo
("il regno dei cieli")
l'universo
potrà
valicare
(come la scimmia e l'atomo)
bàb-baobab-babele
babele
baobab
BAB

starry babs of awareness
open to new identity
Manhattan angular mandala
island
archetypal chrysalis of the metamorphic age
from whence one and threefold
(beyond arrogant babble)
man
may
enter
("the kingdom of heaven")
the universe
(like the monkey and the atom)
bàbbaobabbabel
babel
baobab
BAB

28. Terrestre cifra protesa dal nitore

Terrestre cifra protesa dal nitore
vastità di grappolo e cristallo
stessa sottesa sostanza
all'Indio
usurpata
Nome di colomba e di metallo
aggrappata al Tropico del Cancro
e a sud del Sud nel trepidante freddo
Terra del Fuoco
ed oltre dell'Inverno intatto territorio
d'illimitato azzurro identico anelo
d-onde
Ande memoria minerale
a lande d'insonnia
sudario del sudore
al mormorio fluviale remot-e-manazioni
cascate polifoniche polverizzante
voce
d'uragano
ed altro del qui ed ora nominato
fino
all'uva inquieta dell'Oceano
di tormento e placentare spuma

Finché vento
venne invadendo di sventura
d'identità e orizzonte il patrimonio
d'opprimente infamia
e inferto
inferno
lo stivale di bitume che confonde
addizione con ascesa

Terrestrial cypher unfolding from sharpness

Terrestrial cypher unfolding from sharpness
vastness of cluster and crystal
same subtending substance
from the Indian
usurped
Name of dove and of metal
grappled to the Tropic of Cancer
and south of South in trepidatious cold
Tierra del Fuego
and beyond Winter intact territory
of boundless identical blue I hanker after
waves
Andes mineral memory
to lands of insomnia
shroud of sweat
to fluvial murmuring remote-emanating
polyphonic pulverizing cataracts
voice
of hurricane
and besides the here and now named
as far as the
restless grapes of the Ocean
of torment and placental foam

As long as wind
came invading with adversity
of identity and horizon of heritage
overwhelming shame
and inflicted
hell
the boot of bitumen that confounds
addition with ascent

sventurando
d'astio astuto astenico all'amore
con la refurtiva d'intrighi e dogmi
assoldò
sicari e vili servi il fello
gli occhi sigillando con randelli
perché speranza
dignità
ragione
affondino nell'infinita offesa
della polvere
ombre
divorate
al curvo ciel-o-scuro di delitti
ed
Albe
bandiere insanguinando
in grembo all'astrale curvatura
mosche orbe al molteplice
nell'avaria d'escrementi superstiziosi
avari avvii
ai mutamenti mutili
dell'ombelicale cordone già dal taglio
ed ogno dove
sotterraneo mattatoio dell'assenza
che essenza umana oblii

Mentre del mondo i potenti
della
Veglia
traditori
ricevono assiomatici assassini
tetri rigurgiti di luride latrine
loschi orchi d'arroganti toraci
rachitici

calamitising
with astute hatred asthenic to love
with the loot of intrigue and dogmas
hired
killers and vile servants the felon
sealing eyes with cudgels
that hope
dignity
reason
might sink into the infinite offense
of dust
shadows
devoured
under the curved crime-darkened sky
and
Dawns
bloodstaining flags
in the astral womb fold
flies blinded to the multiple
in the failure of superstitious excrements
beggarly beginnings
of already cut maimed mutations
of the umbilical cord
and every
underground slaughterhouse of absence
that human essence forget

While the powerful of the world
on the
Vigil
receive
traitors
axiomatic killers
dismal spew of filthy latrines
shady orcs with arrogant chests

bardati
pavidi paladini che anche il dubbio deturpano
ma
non le Madri
pazze della piazza
ove la menzogna ha fauci nefande
rospi corazzati del più tetro maschismo
postulanti pustole postribolari
che lordano con lodi vomitevoli
finanche la loro guerra
paria
aporia
della loro pace
desolando con squallide e feroci eiaculazioni
d'ignominiosi stupratori di nuovi lager-gulag
virioni viril-i-mpotenti senza i roghi

Ivi il mio canto
incorruttibile mestruo alare
osa
nel giacimento ove di-a-mante il giorno
avida vita collassare vidi

Inascoltate Madri queste Donne
conobbero Tenerezza Amore Pianto
ora d'angoscia il cuore
palpitante nido assediato
strazio consuma ma non annienta
chi d'aurora irrora n'è irrorato
oltre l'ostile silenzio inascoltate
Dicono
oltre la paura con sguardo nudo
DICONO
agli occhi blindati di funerea pomice
dei boia

stunted
harnessed
pavid paladins which even fearful doubt disfigure
but
not the crazy Mothers
of the square
if the lie has nefarious jaws
armored toads of bleakest machismo
postulant postribular pustules
that soil with vomit-inducing lauds
even their war
aporia
pariah
of their peace
desolating with squalid and fierce ejaculations
of ignominious new lager-gulag rapists
stake-less -him-potent manly hunk-men

There my song
incorruptible menstrual wing
dares
in the diamond-vein of loving day
I saw avid life collapse

Unheard Mothers these Women
knew Tenderness Love Weeping
now with anguished their throbbing
heart besieged nest
torment consumes but does not annihilate
who waters dawn is watered
besides the hostile silence unheard
They say
beyond fear with forthright gaze
THEY SAY
to the eyes armored with funerary pumice

della
Storia
delle luttuose occhiaie grette d'anonimi mostri
d'inermi marionette d'indistinto destino
carnefici che parlano di patria
intendendo la loro prostituta
emblematica
ivi regredire senza trasgredire
DICONO

Udite dalle radici insanguinate
salire
gli
steli
stelle rinasceranno aurorALI
UDITE
annichilendo i Sogni non si h-a-nulla il terrore
chi offende la morte dei nemici
ha rantoli e medaglie depredate nell'udito
non suoni e mutazioni
rantoli
rotolanti nel cranio sotto vuoto
medaglie eclissanti nel vacuo demenziale
odi d'odi o dì

Nessun-o-blio
senza memoria il futuro è simulacro
sotterranea talpa che divora le radici
deperendo dell'umano ogni co-scienza
nessuno oblii del Silenzio
il
GRIDO
Mortali
udite
Qui ed ora elevo l'irto canto

of the henchmen
of
History
of the mournful eye-circles of mean anonymous monsters
of helpless puppets of indistinct petty fate
executioners who speak of homeland
meaning their emblematic
prostitute
where to regress without transgressing
THEY SAY

Hark the bloodstained roots
climbing up
the
stems
aurora-winged stars will be reborn
HARK
by annihilating Dreams terror is not an-nulled
those who offend the death of enemies
death-rattles and pillaged medals in
sounds and mutations
death-rattles
rolling in vacuum-packed skull
eclipsing medals in the madding void
odes of hatred or day

No for-get-full-ness
without memory the future is a simulacrum
underground mole devouring the roots
wasting away all human con-science
no forgetfulness of Silence
the
CRY
Mortals
hark

canto alle Madri che con ninnenanne
o ferma voce figli Vegliarono
VEGLIANO
vegliando alle Donne che amo canto
il sorriso albeggi l'avvenire della Terra
"Oid mortales el grito"
udite
Il
CANTO

Here and now I raise this rugged song
I sing to the Mothers who with lullabies
or firm voice will Kept Vigil over children
KEEP VIGIL
it is vigil over the women that I love to sing
may smiles dawn on the future of the Earth
"Oid mortales el grito"
hark
the
SONG

29. Albania

Albania
veteroblatte irate
senza iride
Tirana
tirannicida
è
l'Alba

Albania

Albania
irate
iris-devoid
age-old cockroaches
tyrannicidal
Tirana
it's
Dawn

30. Ove deriv-ando in-certi segni

Ove deriv-ando in-certi segni
a miseria d'uomo il mondo evolve
ed ulteriore virus mi dolora

Cina Popolare
Primavera
Pechino
luminosi studenti disarmati
figli del futuro
in
Piazza
della Pace Celeste alla morte vi-cina
Per non abiurare il sogno
massacrati

Deng
l'infame Xiaoping
ponga
fine
al suo imbalsasmato cuore incancrenito
e all'immonda cricca
di criminali di pace

Prima-vera
utopia
il volo del volere
del potere
intrighi di ghisa
menzogna
blindate menzogne corazzate
contro le ali della parola
l'incomprensione pianificata dei rackets

Where un-certain signs a-rise

Where un-certain signs a-rise
towards human misery the world evolves
and ulterior virus grieves me

Popular China
Spring
Beijing
luminous unarmed students
children of the future
in the
Square
Of Heavenly Peace close to death
Not to renounce the dream
China massacred

Let Deng
the infamous Xiaoping
put an
end to
his embalmed gangrenous heart
and filthy clique
of criminals of peace

First-spring time-true
utopia
flight of will
for power
intrigues of cast-iron
mendacity
armored plated lies
against wings of words
incomprehension planned by the rackets

degli
usurai
assassini di sempre
ora
manda rinati
di lucertoloni l'armata
da droghe in draghi
trasformati
in armi falli
contro la folla inerme
(non amorfa massa)
i dazebao la carne
i
giacigli
della democrazia nascente
fiere calpestando fiori
i
suoi
orchi
dai grappoli umani
la rossa bandiera del sangue
sradicata
lordando ancora

Nella stagione dei frutti
i cinici feudatari d'oriente
daranno
un rinnovato raccolto
di
miseria

Eppure
banditi
da Tian An Men i banditi
i sinistri pi doc chi

of
usurers
long-lasting assassins
now
sends reborn
armed giant lizards
from drugs to dragons
transformed
into phallic weapons
against the unarmed crowd
(not amorphous mass)
the dazebaos the flesh
the
sleeping places
of nascent democracy
fiends flat-trampling flowers
orcs
human herds
the red flag of blood
rooted
up
soiling once more

In the season of fruits
cynical feudal lords of the East
will provide
a renewed harvest
of
misery

and yet
bandits
from Tian An Men the bandits
those sin-ister lice

dalla criniera del popolo
d'individui
indi
vidi persone
ove derivando in-certi segni

wearing the plumes of the people
of individuals
where
I saw persons
from whom un-certain signs derive

31. Rito scrutando all'orizzonte

Rito scrutando all'orizzonte
il
mare
dal monte aspro
di
sperata
mente
a volte ha volto
sperso speme
speleo
covo nei meandri
tra
marci
tramano
nell'ossimoro mondo
da sempre sequestrato
d'usura eroso
osare
qui
cova
status quo
rovi-ne frantumi smisurati
assolati assoluti
fai-da
te
assioma
assilla assola
timo
ore tra sassi
duttili
relitti

Rite peering at the horizon

Rite peering at the
horizon-distant
sea
from the harsh mount
of
longed for
mind
sometimes has sent
dispersed
hope
delving
den in meanders
amid
rot to
plot
in the oxymoron world
forever seized
by eroding usurer
daring
here
hatching
status quo
bramble-shattered unfathomable ruins
sunny absolute
do-It
yourself
truism
tantalising thirsty
thyme
now mid ductile
stones

del ribellismo della rassegnazione
decade decàde
dell'abbandono nell'immutabile fatalità
non si ha coscienza senza risonanza
eco disfatto vestigia
d'io
di noi sauri
l'imprinting che memora
assomma assonna
assolda
la
barbarie
è
assurdo non l'azzardo
che assurge a quotidiano
ma
l'assuefatto
stato
qui
è
quiete
cava
di rigogliosa morte
da
secoli
annunciata
l'essenza nell'assenza
altro-v-e tutto
l-abile labirinto opposto all'ago
della
bussola
l'ego nella perdita perdura
ac-cadendo moltiplica lapilli
d'assillo l-esil-io

flotsam
of the rebellion of resignation
decade declining
abandonment of immutable fatality
there is no consciousness without resonance
echo defeated remnants
of the ego
of us saurs
memory-impressed
imprint
summing sleepiness
to hired
barbarity
not
the
hazard
claiming normality
is absurd
but
dependent
status
here
is
still
quarry
of luxuriant death
for
centuries
announced
the essence of absence
there is all else
labile-skilled maze against
compass
needle

chi
imbestia
più crudele della bestialità
dei
minotauri sopravvissuti
d'impervio
impeto impietoso
nell'imploso ecosistema
predato
l'archetipo
da claustrofobica insonnia
incube
amnesia inerta
le cento reti della reticenza
nel cosmo che s'espande
cosmesi
alla
lùe
d'umana esiguità
affrontando il nulla
di remoto timore
succube
d'omertà trema
luce svela o acceca
brivida ostaggio
sol-o-mbra
falò faloppa silente
o
urlo randagio sull'orlo
degenerazione
in
gene
razione
scheggia riemersa di rimossa chiarezza

ego loss continues
by-dropping multiplies lapilli
with hassle-hexyl-I
who
bestialises
crueller than the bestiality
of
minotaur survivors
of impervious
impetus merciless
of imploded ecosystem
the archetype
despoiled
by claustrophobic insomnia
incubating
amnesia inerting
the hundred nets of reticence
in the cosmos that expands
cosmetics
a
lues
of human smallness
facing the void
of far-off fear
succubus
of guilty silence trembles
light reveals or blinds
shivers hostage
sun-shadow
bonfire of silent fallopian
or
stray scream on the brink
degeneration
in

che più non fende
offende
senza
rimorso
predestinata preda predatrice
da ingordi gattopardi depredata
ed
oltre
l'abnorme predominio
normalizzante
d'emiciclo cieco strage strazia
rito
scrutando
all'orizzonte il mare
da stremati monti
lì
vidi
calvari
incessanti esìli d'emigranti nati
d'albe incancellate filamenti
cordami vorticosi
subito saio di tramonti
miserere misantropo
fruga
dilaga
spariti uccelli dall'inasprito cielo
ma
dite voi che avete voce
è
il calvario che adonta
o
l'onta
dell'Aspromonte
al

gene
ration generation
resurfaced splinter of removed clarity
which no longer cleaves
offends
without
remorse
predestined preying predator
plundered by greedy ocelots
and
beyond
abnormal normalizing
predominance of the
hemicycle of blind massacre rends
rite
peering at
horizon-distant
sea
from weary mountains
there
I saw
calvaries
incessant exiles of emigrants born
of sunrises unerazed filaments
whirling ropes
immediate sunsets habit
wretched misanthrope
rummages
spreads
birds disappeared from the embittered sky
but
you say that you have voice
it is
the ordeal that sullies

sole
sprone sprona spro-no

or
the shame of
Aspromonte
in the
sun

spur spurring spur-no

32. Acqueo mi acquatto a volte

Acqueo mi acquatto a volte
per misurare il cielo
e
valicarlo
Ionio oinoi
ioni a iosa del primo albeggiare
che
con
passione
compassione
vidi
luogo fecondo
guscio
d'identità
riflettendo nell'altrove
diversità versando pioggia
covo
coeva degli opposti
dolore sconfinato non offusca
somm-e-rgendo di lume la tua cifra
mare amare ogni altro memora
ogni altra terra
dimora
ogni altra luce nutrendomi
di
amante
l'isola del mio cuore ha più del bulbo
radici
iride sciente psicobussola
del dì-verso trasparenza e spuma
ogni altr-a-ria
donde onda e corpuscolo

Aquatic I squat by times

Aquatic I squat by times
to measure the sky
is
over-pass the
Ionian Oinoi
oodles of ions at break of day
that
with
passionate
compassion
I saw as
fecund place
kernel
of identity
reflecting in elsewhere
diversity decanting rain
I brood
coeval of opposites
boundless pain does not obfuscate
sub-merging with light your cypher
sea to love all other recounting
every other land
hosts
every other light feeding me
with
lover
the island of my heart has more
than the bulb
roots
knowing
psycho-compass iris of
day-diverse transparency and foam of

all'alare tuo alito trasalendo ascendo
esule esulto
assola
l'assoluto
brancolante balocco logorando
nel
frangente
fra-nata morte
e raro errare ora colo d'affanni
esorcizzando il tarlo
tu-o-rlo
tuo-no tunnel
d'ogni vivente l'umano il più infelice
inverno invero in ve-rsi
algente guscio m'accolse
nascente
proteso seme alla germinazione
prua
pupilla
e iride all'iridescenza
insite insidie
sfuggendo
spente ginestre
da pruina pruni scheletriti
incur-vita noderosa vite spoglia
néssile
anch'essa in attesa per donare
l'uliv-o-sa
foglie labiali d'enigmatico sorriso
il
pino
némbo d'aghi senza cruna
per non indurre d'arcano monito
il
cammello

every other air
whence wave and corpuscle
to your breath winging wincing I ascend
exiled I rejoice
solo-slotting
the absolute
floundering plaything fraying
in the
breaker's
birth-death glide
and rare errant hour of trickling-trouble
exorcising the woodworm
you hem-yolk
your thunder-tunnel
of all living beings human are unhappiest
winter indeed I in-verse
freezing husk received me
nascent
germination-bent seed
pupil
prow
and iris of iridescent
inherent pitfalls
escaping
from lackluster broom
to blooming skeletal thorns
in curved life-bare knotted
braided vines
waiting too to donate
the
olive-daring
labial leaves of enigmatic smile
the
pine
nimbus of eyeless needles

a remote avventure
tengono tanno attonito
querce
su timpe attempat-e-manazioni
torr-e-nte sillabico
impietriti palpiti perpetui
rugginosi monti il castagno
inerpicando
ciuffo ai rami avvinto
vischio imperla
all'alt-o-rlo biado brado
del biancore di smarrente sale
tendevo dal nadir
verso lo zenit solstiziale
dall'amnio
all'orizzonte
quanto al seno a smisurata luce
tendo più che al senno
all'avverso versi
l-ibri-do
libri
d'onde d'opalescenza mare profilando
funi fiumi fumi
fuso argento sicché secche
fiumare
aculei di cristallo aveva il tempo
geloni l'infanzia
doleva
d'olive diluite al poco pane
ciottoli levigati ed arenili lunari
ove impigliati proni
tronchi
dormivano sculture nell'incanto
derivando
con stormi e s-carni umani

avoiding with mysterious warning to lead the
camel
into remote adventures
they hold astonished tannin-bark
oaks
onto venerable vertigo-reef emanations
syllabic towering-torrent-entity
perpetual petrified palpitations
rusty chestnut mountains
cluster
clinging
to branch-bond
pearly mistletoe adorns
high-hemmed wild-oat
be-wildering sea-salt white
I stretched from nadir
to solstice zenith
from amnion to
horizon
as to the breast to limitless light
I tend more than to wisdom
to adverse verses
cross-bred
tome-hybrids of
whence waves of opalescent sea loom-weave
rope- river fumes
molten spindle-silver so that droughty
stream-lets
time crystal quills made
childhood chilblains
ache from
diluted olives to scarce bread
polished pebbles and lunar sands
where trapped in trunks
slept prone

l'orrendo non arredo
rasserenante
ghigno varco vano della certezza
ne allevo basilischi
basilic-o-nnivoro coltivo
m'acqueo
m'acquatto nu-dandomi all'evento
d'involucri concentrici d'opaco
per amor-ale
amor
non c'è amnistia

bewitched sculptures
deriving
with flocks and de-fleshed humans
horrible non- soothing
furnishing
vain grin –gap of certainty
I breed basilisks
cultivating
omnivorous basilisk-basil
aquatic me
squatting bare-giving myself to the event
of concentric shells of opaque
no amnesty

33. Bast-a-rdi

Bast-a-rdi
d-i-speranza che non spera
VOLA
Vuol Vere Decisioni
forti fatti
fotte intanto del cinismo derisione
fotte d'acutezza spettro appena
fotte tanti
stupra
morte
eroe or ora orrore
or-gia
la barbarie fotte àncora
arcaizzando anninovanta
Urge
e gru del remoto non rimosso
porterà voli an-negati
si sa sassi
pietre
focaie
queste cifre sono massi
di
mas-sacro
profanate dell'umano
abbaiare di sirene fluttua orrendo
sventaglio d'eliche
chele
calamitose
chi no chino inchioda intrigo
rotea
turbinante aria spettrale
foschi

Bast-a-rds

Bast-a-rds
of un-hopeful hope-less-ness
FLIES
Desiring Veritable Decisions
forceful facts
fucking cynicism's derision meanwhile
fucking spectre barely insightfully
fucking many
rapes
death
hero here-and-now horror
or or-gy
fucking barbaric anchor
archaising nineteen nineties
Urges
and crane of remote un-removed
bringing un-drowned flights denied
sage- sapient stones
fire-full
flints
these cyphers are boulders
of
mass- sacred massacre
profaned of the human
siren-barks fluctuating horrendous
propeller- whirr
calamitous
clam-claw
bending the unbent rivets intrigue
rotates
gyrating ghostly air
grim-gloomy

ha
plumbei assedi
ossidi l'attesa nei meandri
salamandre in salamoniche maschere
gregali grugni larvati
senza labbra
lebbra
craniale nell'untuoso pallore
rostr-i-mpassibili d'arrogante ferocia
emorragici pensieri emozioni
annichilite glaciazioni
del
boato
rancido respiro carie killer
il caliginoso rutto tuono teso
all'amnesia
al blackout d'ogni barlume
inserrato ultimo gesto
esto
cominciato già concime
cimento
d'emisfero smisurato
nella sagoma di gesso subissato
estorto battito lapillo
lapidato sangue
solo
n'ebbe nebbia
indelebile
macchia
del fardello desolato
d'un ingombro che d'anélito
fu
corpo
la presenza
dell'assenza riflettendo la sostanza

has
leaden siege
oxidised -bone of waiting in mazes
salamanders in solomonic manic-monkish masks
herded larval grunts
lipless
leprosy
cranial with unctuous pallor
impassable rostra of arrogant ferocity
haemorrhaging thoughts emotions
annihilated glaciations
of the
blast
rancid breath killer caries
the murky thunder-belch bent on
amnesia
the blackout of any glimmer
penned-in ultimate gesture
gest
already become manure
plague
of never-ending hemisphere
in overwhelmed chalk outline
extorted lapilli beat
lapidated blood
alone
had its haze
indelible
macula
of desolate burden
of hindrance which of yearning
was the
body
presence
of absence reflecting the substance

il mattino mattatoio è
senz'Alba
il vincente no avvincente andrà
giulivo
salvo limaccioso coagulo
carne vale
bare
quante
o stato ostaggio
se gretti segreti deretan-o-rrendo
in spalle a groppa e talpa
talché
escrementi deviati
alle menti più vicine
ment
omette omertà
iperbari nell'acquario degli squali
quali squallidi squallenti
enti
entità
vano l'oggi
logistici sputi spoliazioni
tanti
tanatici anelli della tenia
che viscere corrode
di te stato
detestato
oltre oltraggio garantendo
d'ogn-i-pnosi
il meduseo ventre occulto
o
culto
della morte nessun desti
no
nella vita nessun dorma

slaughterhouse morning is
Alba-less
the winner won't go wonder- wielding
whooping
except for slimy clot
meat- worth carnival
how many
coffins
oh hostage state
if hindside-horrifying sordid secrets
piggy-backing and mole-delving
so that
deviated excrement
to neighbour-most minds
may lie
omitting silence
hyperbaric in shark tank
as squalid squalling
agent-
entities
vain present-day
logistic spoliation spittle
many
lethal tapeworm loops
corroding your bowels
you
detested
state
besides ensuring outrage
of omni-hypnotising
occult jelly-fishy belly
or cult
of death let no-one arouse-awaken
no
in life let no-one sleep

orma
norma inerme dell'inerte
l'uomo quando imbestia l'uomo
carcass-a-rsa gabbia vuota
scempio empie era
prigioniera
prigione
d'indis-tinto stato in cui
sito
in CAPACI
capacissimi d'annientare
tare del potere che mai logora
chi
cela
in apnea turato il naso
ogni nesso di iattura vuoto dirci
sta
si
stasi
istantanea
nel folto del frinire
fosse ambra del precario
fossile già splendore estivo
schiuso cavo della mano
interstizi di calura
nel silente trasparire d'invisibili
scintille
forse il giorno che declina
n-era estate di dolore
suolo aperto
maciullato
scheggia
che già vestigia
disseminati
crinali d'insediamenti

step-print
powerless provision of the inert
man bestialising man
carcass-cinder empty cage
unholy havoc
captive era
prison
of vague-tinted state wherein
are sited
in ABLE
all-capable of annihilating
taints of power that never wearies
whoever
conceals
in stop-nosed apnoea
every link of empty mishap telling us
to stay
still
static instant
snapshot as if
in the thick of twitter
amber were of precarious
fossil summer splendour already-here
open hollow of the hand
interstices of heat
in the silent shine of invisible
sparks
perhaps the declining day
was its summer suffering
gaping ground
shattered
shard
already remain-adorns
scattered
ridges of senseless

dissennati
bara è stata
ARA
d'ignita dignità
INDIGNAZIONE
contami
nazione
quante bare bari tanti
in se erti ideologici le tarme
o cianotiche farse ossessive
con parate
con
parole
incomparabili
comprabili
compari
pari
abili
vili
per campare per morire
quante bare ogni stagione
senza infame latitanza
dei
signori
delle mosche
reso l'epos adiposo
meta stasi d'ogni balbuzie
Bà al zebùb
mai più soli sole assoli
desolazione
i mutibitumi
del mediocre normalire
lire
ire
scena oscena

settlements
coffin was the
ARE
of ignited dignity
INDIGNATION
count contaminating
nation
how many cheating coffins
conceal high-flown ideological moths
or cyanotic obsessive farces
with parades
with
un-pareiled
preambles
purchasable
performing
peerless
putrid
paragons
to subsist to die
how many coffins every season
without infamous contumacy
of
lords
of the flies
made the adipose epic
semi-meta-stasis of every stuttering
Babble- Be-el- zebub
never again alone sun shine
desolation
the mute-bitumen
of mediocre norma- lira-ing
lira
ire-exit from
obscene scene of

italiana dell'estate
indi stinto stato desta
d'indistinto
STATO
BASTA

Italian summer
whence in-distinct washed-put state awakens
instinctively
STATE
ENOUGH

34. Di viti e impervia

Di viti e impervia
vita
fra filari
collinare declivio
anfiteatro
d'ossido e lamiere nel bagliore
da mare
appare ancora
ma
ha marmi
l'avico grembo estenuato
più che dal tempo corrosi
d'acide piogge
verbo
vestigia
e le melmose spiagge
l'orda lorda
nega
annega
riverbera il miraggio
Della feccia della Terra
ignari ragni
cavalcando cavallette mercenarie
tra specie in estinzione
e dell'odierno Adamo
In-dio
etnocidio
predano il terrestre patrimonio
scotennano la foresta tropicale
roghi
infernali
d'amnesia nell'Amazzonia

Of vines and impervious

Of vines and impervious
life
twixt trellis rows
hill-sloping
amphitheater
of oxide and iron-sheeted
sea glow
appears again
but
with marble
antic womb worn-out
rather than by time corroded
by acid rain
verb
vestiges
and mucky beaches
the horde soils
denies
drowns
reverberates the mirage
Of the dregs of the Earth
unwitting spiders
riding mercenary grasshoppers
amid endangered species
of today's Adam
Indio-god
ethnocide
prey on the terrestrial heritage
skin-scalping the tropical rainforest
infernal
fires
of amnesia in Amazonia

sempre l'aborigeno
in ostaggio alla miseria
ed altri sortilegi da sentina
presagiti da presbiti
in salotti desolanti
cessi
il loro
piscio diluviale
che siccità deserta
l'humus
ed il germoglio spettra
e disfa nella pietra l'evento
che
Poesia
scolpisce
dagli albori umani
o non sarà d'ira
l'apocalittico dito del divino
a devastare la vastità del mare
a Nord gia-ce in agonia aberrante
d'asfittica bava gialla
ma l'uomo che delira
la sua grettezza avara
vara
morìa senza memoria
e non errore
l'orrore
che
corrode
dell'ozono l'avvolgente sacca planetaria
ma
l'infame
linfa avvilendo vilipende
la fluidità abissale del mistero
degrado

as always the aborigine
hostage of poverty
and other hexing bilge-filled
presaged by presbyters
in salons bleak
cesspools
their
flood piss
drought desertifying
humus
specterifying sprout
and crumbling in stone the event
that
Poesy
sculpts
since the human dawn
or will it be of anger
that divine apocalyptic finger
devastating the vastness of the sea
North-ward-lying there in aberrant agony
of asphyxiating yellow slobber
but the man who raves
launches
his stingy sordidness
memory-less mass-death
not error
the horror
that
corrodes
the planet enveloping ozone sac
but
the infamous
sap defiling vilifies
the fluidity of the abysmal mystery
degradation

in grado
al punto di non ritorno

Di viti e impervia
vita
fra filari
l-eta-mai-o-mologante
vidi
con fusa demenza dilagare

Terrà la Terra
seme
avviluppato pomo
aeriforme
plurimo cristallo palpitante
tumultando
primordiali passioni
mai
sopite
d'edipico complesso si virale
d'essere
l'arsura matricida
di pestilenziali radiazioni
piagato albero della co-scienza
piegato
eredità inaridita
n'ebbe nebbia
il domani dell'oggi
senz'agire
gli anni anni-entano
o
anni-dano

Terrà la Terra
tana d'amore

decline-able
to the point of no return

Of vines and impervious
life
twixt trellis rows
age-old-homologating dung-heaps
I saw
con-fused dementia spread

The Earth shall Hold
seed
enveloped aeriform
pommel
plurime crystal palpitating
tumult-prompting
primordial passions
never
dull-torpored
by Oedipus complex so viral
to be
matricidal thirst-burn
of pestilential radiation
wound-bearing tree of co-science
bent
withered heritage
fog-possessed
tomorrow of today
inactive
year-annihilating
or
year-lurking years

The Earth shall Hold
lair of love

o
tanatico
covo

Terrà la Terra
seno
vulnerabile al disamore
che con graffio
calanchico
deserta

Terrà la Terra
Eden
in cui nato
l'Uomo

Terrà la Terra

or
deathly
den

The Earth shall Hold
breast
vulnerable to disaffection
which with gorging
goring
deserts

The Earth shall Hold

The Earth shall Hold

35. Migratori

Migratori
uccelli in cielo vedo
aprendo
apprendo
della noce della brina il frutto
si discioglie la notte
si
dilegua
di labirinto non sono
madrepora del cosmo della mente
né collassante caos
queste demenziali esalazioni
in cui nato
miraggio
di realtà sedative
o
messianiche
lino
lenente
fantasmali complessi
nave nàvera viaggiante
liberatoria
fè
feudo
del giocatore del gioco e della regola
no al Tènaro
alla caverna della parola
torno
con colore segno veglia
dall'abissale
specchio
senza ossidiana o diossina

Migratory

Migratory
birds in the sky I spy
opening
I learn
of the nut the frost the fruit
night melts away
fade-
vanishing
of labyrinth I am no
madrepore of the mind's cosmos
nor collapsing chaos
these dementing fumes
wherein is born
mirage
of sedative reality
or
messianic
lenitive
linen
phantasmal complex
clipping clipper voyaging
liberating
faith
fief
of gaming gamester and rule
no to Taenáros
to the cave of the word
I return
with color signing vigil
from abysmal
mirror
obsidian- or dioxin-less

da desolatrici piogge riparo non ebbi
d'arca
alcuna
soffrono le mie mani
frustrante umidità remota
l'esistere
ha tante esche
artiglio in ogni polpa
cela trame efficaci
non sono uccello che canta
i
suoi
domini
NO
non è babelico pene il mio pennello
la mia penna dell'inutile
né della mia vigna ostacolo
la
cuspide
ed il vulcano meno mi dolora
dell'istante che alle tempie
tempestio di fangaia
tonfa
scava tarma
del battito latomia in ogni latitudine
dominatore no sono di me
né
servo
o incagliato cleptomane autodidatta
che colpisce in clessidre
fossili eclissi d'eternità
desvivendo
sua morte dilatata
Arianna del filo della tua voce
nelle

I had no shelter from desolating rains
of ark
at all
my hands suffer
frustrating remote moisture
existence
has many lures
claw in every pulp
hides effective textures
I am no bird singing
its
his
dominions
NO
no babel penis is my brush
my pen of the useless
nor of my vine I hinder
the
cusp
and the volcano grieves me less than
the instant when in temples
quagmire hail
thuds
digs moth-bites
quarry-beat at every latitude
dominator not of me
nor
slave
nor self-taught tangled kleptomaniac
hitting in hourglasses
fossil eclipses of eternity
unliving
her dilated death
Ariadne of the thread of your voice
in

circonvoluzioni
dei miei polpastrelli
succede
seta virtuale
affiora
nonostante l'ignoranza mia
so chi sono ora
piramide m'impedisce
catartico
cattare
e gotici aculei
infangano o infiammano la fronte
che
si
pensa
senza frontiera marea
mi deriva
non
sconfigge
uccelli migratori in cielo
vedo
seme di spazio
e di tempo radice
qui
quia
caduto
incompiuto in divenire
migratore

convolutions
my fingertips
virtual silk
follows
surfaces
despite my ignorance
I know who I am now
the pyramid prevents me
cathartic
plumb
and gothic spikes
besmirch or inflame the forehead
that
one
thinks
border-less tide
drifts me
not
defeats
migratory birds in the sky
I see
seed of space
and root of time
here
therefore
fallen
unfinished in becoming
migratory

36. O d i se ha

O d i se ha
la
vita
senso ancora
d-atomi
e galassie l'avo ignora
partì da particelle elementari
assiderato siderale
e-s-odo
dell'eden utero primevo
espulso
ed
ora
miliardi
di miliardi di miliardi
della complessità sbalorditiva
placenta l'atmosfera
d'emersa
sfera
di cosmica fertilità
non
cedo
eccedo
l'universo di sé coscienza trova

Odd is see if

Odd is see if
life still
possesses a
sense
of atoms
and galaxies to avus unknown
from elementary
stark-ice sidereal particles
de-parting ex-ode
from Eden's primeval womb
expelled
and
now
billions
of billions of billions
of bewildering complexity
placenta the atmosphere
of emerged
sphere
of cosmic fertility
I do not
cede
but exceed
the universe finds conscience of self

37. La scia l'ascia lascia

La scia l'ascia lascia
d'impalpabil-i-ndizi
inesorabili
nell'aria
va
arco
varco
aprendo
eco di sorda tosse
distingue
estingue
ad ogni morso incuneandosi
assenza stessa
estesa
ed anche la quercia
l'Albero
vacilla prima o poi
ma se non cade
è
l'Archetipo

The camber cleaver carves

The camber cleaver carves
impalpable-clues
inexorable
in the air
goes
arc-arching
gape-gapping
throw-opening
echo of hollow hack
distinguishes
extinguishes
at every gash wedging into
absence itself
extended
and even the oak
the Tree
falters sooner or later
but if it fails to fall it
is
the Archetype

Ebr-e-rbe
nell'assedio d'esistere
finché
presente accade
o da ruminanti brucate ancor germogli
bruciate dalla brina
sradicate dal vomere
avvelenate
dai diserbanti
nel letargo dei semi
senza quiete né affanno
il
futuro
nella dissoluzione del grano
per la spiga
già da rugiada giada
solare
generando

Head-y herbs

Head-y-herbs
in the siege of survival
till
the present occurs
or as ruminants you still graze
frost-burnt
shoots
uprooted by the ploughshare
poisoned
by herbicides
during restless stressless
seed lethargy
the
future
in the dissolution of the corn
already
sun-generating
into
jade-be-dewed ear

39. Analfabeta d'innumeri alfabeti

Analfabeta d'innumeri alfabeti
del mattin-o-scillante passerio
mi
sorprende
nel vertiginoso tutto
per
dirsi
perdersi
per
darsi
del nulla nel risucchio
di demoni e dei a fuoco l'artifizio
invano nomando vanno voci
affabulanti architetture
archi
in preda a un sogno
tu in me a chi fai le fusa
d'iride ridà
lucòre
è
giorno
telaio che compatta filo
a
filo
così l'uccello va tessendo il cielo
vivo l'azzurro vive nel suo volo
sul
ciglio
del recint-o-rizzonte stagliandosi
nello spazi-o-sa
l'umano
forse l'induce sapere d'ignorare

Illiterate in countless alphabets

Illiterate in countless alphabets
the morning-oscillating sparrow-twitter
surprises
me
in head-whirling whole
to
say oneself
lose oneself
to
give oneself
the undertow-nothingness
of firework demons and gods artifice
in vain voices go vagabonding
affabulating architectures
arches
prey to a dream
you in me to whom you purr
iris restoring
glow
is
day
loom-compacting thread
to
thread
so the bird may weave the sky
I live the azure living in his flight
on
the edge of
the fence-horizon silhouette-outlined
in the spacious space-dare
the human
inducing him maybe to know he ignores

l'ignoranza
la colpa ed il castigo
analfabeta d'innumeri alfabeti
del mattin-o-scillante passerio
da
nottivaghi
incursioni talvolta nella resa
d'iride ridente lucore
cuore mi tonfa

ignorance
the fault and punishment
illiterate in countless alphabets
the morning-swaying night-wander-worthy sparrow-twitter
incursions by times
surrendering to
of iris laughing heart glow
I thump-thud

40. Pittura ruttil

Pittura ruttil
                è
                        precursore
                                        eros o
                                        erosione
iride-scente innesco
                        innesto
                        innatural
                                        e
                                tra
                                        vitArte
inestricabilmente
                                Evento
                        mente
                icaria
in
    estri
                semi
                        osi
                            in
                                spiga
                        dispiega
                                        originant-e-spandersi
costellando
germinal-e-nergia
                            semmai
                            sema
                                    antica
                                            del
                                                futuro
                                                        o
prematuro passato

Ruptile painting

Ruptile painting
                    useful
                       precursor
                                        eros or
                                        erosion
rain-bow-ful inciting
                  unnatural
                      implant
                            and
                                  twixt
                                     lifeArt
inextricable
               Event
         mental
       icaria
in
   excited
        seeds
             dare
             disclose
                   in
                   sprout
                   spawn -and - spread
constellating
germinal-energy
                          else eras-old
                                  signal
                                     of
                                        future
                                           or
premature past

diaframma
di
        frammentaria
                    rifrazione
                          emisferi

                                        sferri polisemico
                                    sfavill-io
di vibratile g-uscio
iato
        aereo conio
                    o
                    di
                    goccia
                            sedimenti
                                dimensionale
                                dimenìo
                                        o fantomatica

ealtà
        avara
        avrà emarginazione
                            se
                                questo fantoccio
                    umano sequestro
rea
    alta
            dolente o nolent-e-mergenza
                                            non
                                            fondale
né schermo del provvisorio
                            oltre
                                intasamento
                                        mentale
in
    posta

diaphragm
of
 fragmentary
            refraction
                    hemispheres
                        striking
                            polysemic
                            spark
of vibratile sh-shell
    airy coined
                hiatus
        or
                dimensional
            sediments
        of squirming
                drop-let
                    or phantasmal

 miserly
    excluding
     reality
            should
                        this pawn
                human hostage
delinquent
        high
            painful or un-wilful-emergence-y
                            neither
                            backdrop
nor screen of the provisional
                        past
                        mental
                                glut
in
unspoken

impronta
impronunciata
                    folgorando
                                        d'emozionale spazio
sostanza inconscia
            in
                        coscienza
                                    c-osmo-si
                                                traluce
                                                memoria
visionarietà
d'urgenza percettiva
                                    il
                                    dato
                                    antropomorfico
                                    nell'evocativo dilatarsi
dal
punto
alla sfera
            plurimo l'UNO
                                        identifica mutazioni
scaturite d'aneliti
sconvolto l'euclideo piano
                                    del
                                    supporto
superficiale assenza
                        in
                            pelle
                                dosa
                                            profondità
                        impelle
                essenza
enucleando
non
    clonando in vitr-o-rtivo

ventured
vestige
            fulgurating with
                        emotional space
unaware substance
in
      aware
            c-osmos-is
                        transluces
                        remembered
visionary-ness
of perceptive urgency
                        the
                        anthropomorphic
                        datum
                        in evocative dilation
from
point
to sphere
            multiple ONE
                        identifies mutations
sprung from yearnings
upheaving Euclidean plane
                        of
                        supporting
superficial absence
                  in
                        pelt
                        doses
                        depth
                        impelling
                        essence
enucleating
not
      cloning in vitreous-hortive

né

d'azione specchio

larvale

linfa

d'infinito

nel farsi spazio

il

tempo

relativ-o

vital-è

impalpabile precorrimento

germinale

gesto

plasma

plasma d'inesplorato

folgorant-e-mana

s'è

alare

solare

solitudine

da uomini e dei

epigoni

sgomento già bambino

licheni

nitore

nell'impietrito

magm-a-ffiorando

lento

è il tempo

s'umana misura

T-erra

v-erro anch'io

poi

che d'amorfo

offro

                    nor
                action-mirror
larval
lymph of ever-lasting
                space-making
                            relative
                                time
is
        vital
                impalpable precursion or
germinal
gesture
plotting
            unexplored
                plasma
                    fulgurating-emanates
if it be
        soaring
        solar
        solitude
                    of men and gods
                            epigones
amazed from childhood
                        lichen
                        lustre
                            in petrified
magma-stroking
                    slow
                    time
measure
Err-th
bo-err I too
            then of
            amorphous
                offer

senso

al

Fare

ardendo antesi

molecolare

alare

color

entimematico propizi

il percepire

ematico

materico

se

di

mentale universo

nell'avverarsi

som-mo-vimento palpita

in

fluire

atemporale

volto

d'ascolto

oscuro

o scori

scoria

alogica cigola

arente idolatria

triade

tre

volte

travolte

trovate d'epiloganti

ilar-e-segesi

inali dilani

eppur

                        sense to
                                D-eed
                        humanising
ardent molecular
                winged
                sprung
                color
                        entimematic favouring
                                        perception

                        haematic
                                material
                                        if
                                        of
                                        mental universe
in becoming
        com-motion palpitates
                                in
                                a-temporal
                                        flow
towards
audition of
                obscure
                        or
                a-logical
                        littering
                        litter barks
                                ardent idolatry
                                        triad
                                        three
                                                turned
upturned
        twists of hilar-ex-egesis
                                inhale hack
yet

erede vedere
                    non
            è
            né mappare
conflitto
    flippato
            o
    flint
        pire inducendo
percepire
        esige
        si
            gene
            genesi
                        d'indistinto partendo
        tendo
        endo
        ento
        eso
                    indi
                    stinto patendo
                        passi-vita
virulenta velleitarietà
di mediocre
            e
        vacua
            azione
                    patalogia non
                    patos
                    portento
altrimenti
altri
    mentiranno
            ottuso
            o pro-filo

seeing heir
              is not
         either mapping
  flipped
conflict
          or
       pyre-inducing
     flint
to perceive
       extorts

              innate declination
                      inclines
                           endo-
                           ento-
                           eso-

            whence in-
                 distinct patient
              passi-vi-ity
  vicious worthlessness
of mediocre
         and
            vacuous
            action

                    pathology not
                    portentous
                    pathos
otherwise
others
    will merit
           obtuse
                or pro-file

                                        appunto
                                        punto
oltre
    il nero quadrato
                            di Malevič
i ponti arsi nel
        farsi
            si dà o
            si danna l'Arte
                        con

                                        passione
                                compassione
quotidiano pane
                    linfa o
                    infame
                    infanticid-io
                                    siderale
                                    drago squama
selvosa notte peculiare
morfologia
        già
            di
            domani
                    o
                    ebro s'assorbe
albore
    ore
        bla
        bl-a-lbero
                    suono
                        di-vento
                                organo
                                    onagro
                    ragli
in

                         prompt
                         point
beyond
        the black square
                    of Malevič
the burnt bridges in
     becoming
     defer to or
     damage Art
                 with
                     compassionate
                     passion
daily bread
            lymph or
            infamous
            infant-I-cidal
                        sidereal
                        dragon scales
sylvan night peculiar
morphology
        of
        to
            morrow
          or
                 drunk absorbs the
daybreak
    hours
          bla
          bla-treeing
                     sound of
                         organ-becoming
                     wheezing
                     wind

  braying

b
 h
   alba black-out
            dell'umano scemario
                 scene
                 oscene
supposte sponde
opposte
opprime o poi
          x
           fino l'omega
           finisce
               la
                vit-a-ccende o
                 acceca
tabula rasa
    tra
       scendere
            e assalire
      trascende
           preverbale gemmeo
               gesto
                  verso
           proverbiale
               tu
                me
                  fatta
                materia
folgorante anim-a-llatta
          oniric-a-ntimateria
lapsus
lapillare
lapislazzuli
     lì
   azzardo

in
  b
    h
      dawn black-out
                          of inane human
                          obscene
                              scene
supposed
  opposed shores
  oppress or then
                      x
                  to omega
                    ends
                          life- ignites or
                          un-eyes
tabula rasa
              amid
                  descent
                              and assault
                  transcends
                          preverbal gemlike
                                  gesture
                                              towards
                  proverbial
                          tumified
                              you
                                made
                                me
matter
fulgurant soul-nourishing animal
                          oneiric anti-matter
lapillary
lapislazzuli
lapsus
          where

ardo
dò
d'opacità
corpo
rea
ansia
scansione sdensa
sgravi
danza
in-quiete
onde
corpuscolar
fluire
all'episodico
dico
vis
s'esso
ossessivo
intimo il-limite
lì
sta
l'istante
antélio estremo sond-i-ndizio
svampa
d'acceso tizzo in aria
folgor-a-zione
decodifi-canti
in germe
d'io
DNA
apnòico diss-odo la mia vita
qual
or
ali
suoni

glowingly
exposing I
bestow
opacity on
body
anxious blame
un-thickens scansion
un-burdens
dance
un-quiet whence
corpuscular
wave flow
episodically
say I
vis
if
bsessive
intimate un-limit-ness
lies
there

the instant
anthelium extreme probe-clue
glows
of burning ember in air
fulgur-action
decode-if-chant
in germ
of egoic
DNA
apnoeic I crumb-bell up my life
as
wing
word
sounds

d-atomi
palpitando
baleno d'ineludibil provvisorietà
svelante sogno della veglia

            il

              Segno

stami

    in

      ali

         intenso

         intesse d'immerso

            immenso

              Evento

enucleare
da nodale nulla

         so

           già

             c'e

                nel soggetto

                  oggetto mancante

            te

             nera

         materia

interstellare
interstiziale notte dei tempi

              senza cielo

        dei

          spazi-ando

               specie

       grappoli di

       grappoli

doriginari-a-ndroginia
impasto

in

of atoms
palpitating
flash of inescapable impermanence
revealing dream of arousing
                              the
                                        Sign
Stamen
       in
          haling
              intense
              interweave of immersed
                          immense
                                        Event
enucleating
from nodal nothing
                     I know
                          already that
                                   in the subject
                                        lies the missing
                                                   object
                                                             tender
                                                             black
interstellar   matter
interstitial night of skyless
                          times of the
                     gods of
                        space-walking
                              species clusters
of
                          clusters
of
original- and-rogyny
dough

en

pasto l'acino
        l'unico
                argine denigra
                        enigma
                                impeto
                                in
                                        petto
sprofondando risplende
del vuoto
        volto incorporeo
                incorporare
                        raro
                                già
                                        ciglio
                                                oniro
                                                        ironica lavagna
                                                                lava
                                                                latente
                                                                        tentazione
d'eclissi
        clessidri
                impari flare
                        flagrante
                        flus-so-noro
                                                fulcro
                in
                        parola
                        paradigma
                                        gordiano
                                                ombelicale
d'enzimale silenzio
monismo
                        non
                ismo
                        c-osmo-si

dowing seedling
    sole
        buffer denigrates
           enigma
                impetus in
                    pectore
sinking
the incorporeal visage
    of the void shines
  incorporating

        rare
          remote
            edge
                oneiric
                  ironic slate
                    latent
                    lava
temptation
of eclipses
  clepsydra
        inequitable flagrant
           flare
        so-nar-flux
           fulchrum
      in
     phrasal
     paradigm
          Gordian
             umbilical
of enzymal silence
monism
     non
ism
   c-osmos-is

diluire
dilu
vi
di
imperceptibil
stessa
estesa
placent-a-ria
fenice
inarrestabil
mente
cerch-io
P
teco
o trovo
pupillare soglia
d'occhi nudi urge
emozione o
rimozion
è cristallo
stallo
o
sudario
sudditanza
di specchio guscio incrini
in
crisi
crisalide di Senso
Libro
d'unica pagina
anim-a-ccorpa
e
qui
in
ozio

dilute

de

luge

of

imperceptible

self

stretch

placental-air
phoenix

unceasing

ly

eye-seek

P

teque

or find

pupil threshold
of bare eyes urge

emotion or

removal

is crystal

stalling

or

shroud
subject-stance
crack the mirror shell

in

chrysalis
climax of Sense

Book

of one-page

body-soul-whole

and

in

idleness

d'informe
linfa nel
  farsi
     memori-a-neliti o
      moria
         te
          ne
            ebra
         tenebra
                  irrita chi squarcia
proteiforme
       non ammass-a-ssomma
       non compendia
       non deforma né conforma
s'inoltra
compenetrando
         o marginalità
         mar
          argina
            alità
          residuali frammenti
ferite inferte
      ferale atro
        atroce
in
  fertil
    lì
      feraci sementi
        segment-i-mpulsando
esorbitanti
congiunzioni
      levar-si-llab-e-ssenziali
        sibila sericeo
           disinibito
           ibis

of shapeless
sap in
self-make

      memory-a- longing or
        mortality
            be
              drunken
              darkness
                  irks whoever rending
     not sum-mass-ing
     not abridging
     not deforming not conforming
proteiform
enters
penetrating

     or
       marring
       marginal
        anginal
           wind-wing
      residual fragments
inflicted gashes
     feral gloom
       grim
un
  fruitful
     there
       bountiful seedlings
          segment-impelling
exorbitant
conjunctions
      un-syllable-essential
    sericeous sibyl
         uninhibited
          ibis

Antesignano

    Duchamp a scacchi gioca

           va

            allora

       chi

      scaccol-a-ncòra

         àncora

d'Artemide a Efeso

     il tempio al rogo

Eerostrato dà

  strato a

  strato dada

    ante litteram l'arrogante

        e

chimer-e-ffigi-e-ffimere

     in

      mond-o-dierno

post-avanguardie

    e ladri trans-i-tori

       inani sette

tangenziale

promiscuit-a-gonistica

     d'erinni

      impatto

       attonito

        o

in-finito

  nitor-e-rotico

    ere

    si

   e

     l'attimo

la

  cera

lacer-a-cqua

Forerunning
>   Duchamp plays chess
>   where
>   fore
>   winners are
>   those who still
>   snot-pick
Artemis's anchor at Ephesus
>   the temple burnt down
> Herostratus provides
>   stratum to
dada stratum
>   ante-litteram arrogant
>   and
fleeting-chimera-effigy
>   in
>   present-day
post-avant-garde
>   the trans-i-tory
>   inane seven-dwarf sects
tangential
promiscuous-agonistic
>   of erynian
>   shock
>   stunned
>   or
in-finite
>   neat-erotic
>   here
>   s
>   ies
>   the twinkling
the
>   wax
>   water-rends

          qua convulsa
              vulva
                    recondita mutazione
decomposizione in
     composizione
                d'anaptissi
                          ibridi
                    equilibri
assimilare
            non
            rende
     simile
          dà intensità
                    all'intuizione inducendo
                    al presente
                              il
                                 futuro
palindroma odissea
rappresi
     esistenziali
                grumi
                agrum-i-nusitati
                     umici
                agrori
                          da
                              morsura
                                        lis-e-silità
lapidato lapillare barlume
delitti perpetrati nei meandri
                              vestigia
                                   già
                              vesti
ogni altro dato
          tolto
                crocevia non ha

present convulse
vulva
recondite mutation
decomposition in
composition
of hybrid
anaptyxis
equilibriums
not assimilating
rendering
similar
bestows intensity
on intuition inducing
to the present

the
future
palindrome odyssey
coagulated
existential
congeals
un-usual citruses
humic
bitterness
of
biting
worn-out exility

lapidated lapillary glint
crimes perpetrated in meanders
already vested
vestiges
all other datum
taken
history has no

               la
               storia
        croce
          vi
            ha ogniqualvolta
in
  certi
incert-i-nghiottitoi
          civiltà
           vilt-a-vvolge
                divora
ogniqualdove
       e
      p
        t-affi-ora
           disse
             polta
calvo
    rio
      trama ruvida
         a dirupo
            ora
             colare
inedi o
inedito d'energia greme
        emerg-a-ssetata esattezza
                 ab-ovo
germi
    in
      azione
        urgenza
          al quia
           altrove adeso
             adesso
nel dar luogo al non

crossroads
cross
there
is
ever
in
certain
uncertain-swallowing
civilisation
is vile-evolved
devouring
every time
e
pi
tap-h-our
dis
interrered
cal
vary
rough plotted
precipice
now
pouring
hungry or hilt-full of novel energy
emerging exactitude-thirst
ab-ovo
germs

in
action
urgency
wherefore
elsewhere now
adhered
in making place to non

luogo
    t'amerò mero remoto
           ovunque
                sussulto
rivolo
 volo
 volto frale
    fra
    le
      doglie
      tornasole
          qual quantico quipu
s-offro
    do
      loro
        nudo presente
        nodo
          vegli
         grovigli neuronali
               esodo
               odo
                  se
formi
   col
     io
        acm-e-idetico
        ele-mentale verifica
            carnale
perdita
gravitazional
     è
        migrante memoria
          meta-morfica
             cifra
          midollare

place
      I will love you mere remote
        anywhere
start
filter
flight
frail face
    mid
      pangs
      litmus
        as quantic quipu
I suffer-offer
    give
      them
        nude present
        node
          waking
        neuronal webs
          exodus
           hearing
         whether
ting
  ling
    I
    acme-eidetic
    elemental-mental
       verify carnal
loss
gravitational
     is
      migrant meta-phoric
       memory
marrow
         cipher
prodromes

prodromi
     i
       soli
          approdi
sostanzi-alita
ma chi non veglia
          men
            sogna
          menzogna falsarosauro
d'elucubrazioni
     abrasioni
         blo-b-ulimici
           cinici
           cincischiamenti
zepping
zadanovismo
    nuovismo esiguo appena
        happening
            zavorra
            vorr-a-rrovellare
non emblematico shock
       shopping ad hoc
     lo show
ciarliero
ciarpame postrémo
       disse
        astro
          il
           dito
arte-rio-sclerotico
       dopante tangenzialità
        tange o
        tacita
          ignavia non
          ignente via né

the
         sole
substance-breathing
              landings

but the unaware
                 un
                      truth dream
                      untruth sham-o-saur
of lucubrations
          abrasions
                      blob- bulimic
                                mocking mumbling

zepping
zadanovism
       newism slim hapless
                  happening
                              weighty

wilful-wisp- wishing
un-emblematic shock
          ad hoc shopping
                  showy
gabbling
garbage postremus
                      dis
                           aster
                                the
art-erio-sclerotic finger
                      doping tangent
                         touches or
                         hushes
             apathy neither
             igniting path nor

  agnosia

                                    lambì

                                    ambigua

                                        iguana

artefare

        è afasico

            afelio

                        non

        fare

Arte

            questione

            quest-a-spirando

                        spirali

                        ali

                        li volo

                            o

                            onta

                    volontà d'albero

                                d'albe

                                        plasma

osmotico sorriso

                        ogni dove amletico

                            anelito

                                    al

                                    presente

                                    mancante

non arcaico avvenirismo

                            smorfia

lai

        globale la bolgia

                        al

                        albume

                        abbandoni

                                don-i-nducenti

o speculare supporto

                anguish

                    brush

                        ambiguous

                            iguana

artmaking

     is asphyxiating

       aphelion

              not

   making

Art

    question

    quest-inspiring

       spiral

      soars

        in flight

       or

      mar

       arboreal will

      to shape

     dawns

osmotic smile

      everywhere Hamletic

       yearning

          present

          day

          lack

no archaic ground-breaking

         sneer

lays

    global the albumen

       bedlam

       abandoning

       gift-inducing

or specular support

concentric-i-noltr-a-rsi

                            secreti

                            segreti o

                            se

                                greti

                                    ingressi di

                                        grassume

                                            assume

d'appet-iti-neranti

anoressi-rabdomanti-che vestali

        esse

                oss-a-ssetati flauti afflitti

                                            fianchi

                                            palestrati

astenico candore da candeggio

s'orda

sorda

        a suggello greggio gergo

                    gregaria caterva

                                        cita

                                    fagocita viatico

tonfa

        affonda

                a tetri detriti

                        in men che non si dica

                            mena

                            meningi

                                inarca crani

e

    qui

        va

            lenza

                all'amo

                        pio bove

                                osservi

concentric-in-trusion
secreting
secrets or
should
gravelled
entrance to
greasiness
assume
of inherent appetites
anorexic-water-divining vestals
their
obsessive-bone flutes afflicted
aerobic
flanks
asthenic bleached candour
horde
unhearing
endorsing flock jargon
flocking swarm
quoting
phagocitising viaticum
thud
sinks
to grim garbage
in a blink
bending
brains
stooping skulls
e qui
valent
link
to
hook
gentle ox
observing

o servi dela-tori e

amenze mucche
ammucchi di neve

qual d'astinenza sputi

mucido mugghio

sponda
risponda di-l-aghi

dalla cruna

nel pagliaio

cospicu-i-ncrementi
escrementizi

odi

insediarsi
in
sé
di
arsi e qui

voco
orlo d'urlo
o
mero

di
vino primevo preme

col
mare
colmare
in
ogni
goccia

mole
cola
colà

eppur-e-ruppe
aurorale gioia

or serving dilating-bull and

cowing amentia

cairns of snow

as abstaining spits

mouldy bellow

resort

retorts dilating needle

in haystack

conspicuous increments excremental

hatred

installs itself

in

self

of

ardent e qui

vocal

edge of yell

or

mere

di

vine primeval press

to

swell

the waves

with

every

drop

molecule

percolate

where

still erupts

auroral joy

d'amor
           veemenza precoce o
           emenza prematura
                   orbate
lingua
inguine ardente vuol
             e
             di
              po
                il prima
azzarda
    arda orizzonte
          infino
          infinitezz-a-zzerante
fetale
       folgorando
          improvviso
          improvvisazione non è
                né
fatale smidollo di successo
mucillaginoso rigurgito d'oblio
              ribalta la
              ribalta
lode
     lisc-a-ddesca
         scadute merci
           mercimon-i-mperterriti
               riti
              irretire
ipnotici
atterrenti torren-tizi e cai-ni
imperversano
          solerti tre los-chi
              chini
              inibiti bini

of love
            precocious vehemence or
            premature eminence
                                    deprived
tongue
seeks fiery groin
                        oe
                    di
                        pus
                            first
dares
  ardent horizon
                as far as
                        foetal
                zero-infinity
            fulgurating
                        unprompted
                        inventiveness is
                                        neither
fatal gutless success-crave
slimy regurgitation of oblivion
                            upsets the
                            set
praises
        fishbone-allure
                    expired goods
                        reckless simoniac
                                    rites
                                    netting
hypnotic
terrifying torrent-types and Cains
rampaging
            bent on shifty
            bending
                    inhibited binary

degrado in
grado
     inabissati nel rimosso
                  esizial
                  esito
                     o
mani
    come
       ali
         vortico
           oso
              ci
                trovo
                    l'inafferrabile
simultaneità sintagmatica
d'obliquo
  oblio
  oblò la cenere
          del
          fuoco
              ama
                alga
                   mare
occupa
  cupa
     opaca
       canapa
           e grev-e-rge
                aire
                    juta
hic et nunc
      lievita
      lì
      è
        vita

filth fit to
          sink into
remorse
                              commonplace
                              outcome
                                   or
hands
     like
          wings
               daring
                    vortex
                         there
                              I find
                                   the
                                        ungraspable
  syntagmatic simultaneousness
of oblique
     oblivion
     doused the ashes
                         of the
                         fire
                              am
                                   alga
                                        mate
dwell in
drab
          opaque
               hemp
                    and grave
                         heaved
                                   jute
hic et nunc
               rises
               where
                    life

collassante

    percezione

        esito

        e

        sito

        situa

          azione

d'irrazional

  irradiazione induce

      tra

        fitta

        finitezza

       sfinge

         ingenerante

        in

         gente

            civiltà o

            viltà

dapprima dei metalli

  prioritaria

    al progresso

        allarma

        all'Armonia

dall'insignificanza

al

sublime

    ruttil-e-ppur

      Pittura

is
collapsing
perception
achievement
and
site
situation
of irrational
irradiation induces
mid
dazing
density
sphinx
generating
gar
gantuan
civility or
vileness
primarily of metals
priority
of progress
alarms
Harmony
from insignificance
to
sublime
ruptile
yet pure
Painting

41. Minuscolo frammento

Minuscolo frammento
          fra mento e cranio
                    amni-o-ceano
lapislazzul-i-lozoistico
lapillar
          ingemmi
          in
               nardi
                ardi
                di
                         minerali
                              aligeri
                                        l'immenso
d'io
          singolare pluralità
                         alita
                              battiti scavando
m-istero
               x
                    plesso
                         solare
                              nel Fare
                                        so-ggetto non
                                        soggiaccio
                              nel fatto
                                   né
                                        in
                                             platoni-ca-verna
                                                  vernale punto
se
     mente
semente

Minuscule fragment

Minuscule fragment
       midst chin and cranium
            amni-o-cean
lapislazzul-i-lozoistic
lapillary
       in-gemming
       in-
        censing
        scents
           of
              winged
                 minerals
                    the immensity of
ego's
singular plurality
       breathing
          delving pulsations
m-hysteric
     solar
        per
          plexus
             Making
                sub-ject not
                sub-mitting
           in fact
              or
               in
                 vernal
            platonic-cave
            point
were
wits to

seme
se
  me
      osi
        corpo
          or
           alita
             oltre l'organico
                 vision
                   è
                     l'urgenza
intatte le ginocchia
solamente
o
d'unico
      dittico
         trittico
           alien-a-zion
                e
infimo
infino di squallidi
        idilli
          tetro
            aedo
              o
          tersa
            dimensione
odissea
    a
      essi
        do
          non dolo l'aporia
            o
             lodo
              odierno

wield
    seed
where
  the body
      dares
          now to
             breathe
             beyond organic
                  vision
                  is
                     urgency
intact the knees
only
or
sole
    diptych
        triptych
          alien-action
             and
deepest
ditch of squalid
      idylls
        dim
        dwelling
           or
        unsullied
         odyssean
          dimension
to
   these
     I give
       not deceiving doubt
         or
          praise
           today

do

lor

ordalico né

ordinario ma

guad-a-nabasi

intimo

timico

intimpa

voce

in

canti

primordiali

ali

ordi

primo

amigdala d'ossidiana

diana

d'inedito

o

inedi

di

lieve

sorriso

immensurabil

è

alfa

alfin ingente

d'ignoto

scarabocchi fulminei

occhi

sinapsici

sinolo

o giaci cristallo

stallo

ti conformi

I deal
            them neither
     ordeal nor the
     ordinary but
ford-an-abisis
          intimate
            thymus give
          booming
                    voice
                         in en-
                              chanting
                                   primordial
                                        wings
                                        weaving
                              primal
amygdale of obsidian
               glow
          unknown
        or slight
starved
smile
immensurable
              is
           alpha
             against huge
                              unknown
fleeting scribbles
          eyes
         synapses
         synolon
                or
                 else
                  lie a stalled
                  crystal
                     you conform

tormento
fermento
                non
fermi
        di
                amante
                        esul-e-stuoso
                                        demon
                                            nome
l'inaccessibil
    accende
                lato
                alato
                    oltre sfera
                                fiat
                                fiato
                                    il
                                    soffio
                                    risonanza
qual dei miei albori
            d'albicocca dal nocciolo
                                        molato
                                        immolato
midollo
sem-e-spulso
                da parallelo buco
                            n'ero
                                stupito
cass-a-rmonica
                in
                vortice
                clessidra
                        d'afasia
                            al dire
                                    o

torment
ferment
          not
firm
      diamond
          loving
                  exile fiery
                      demon
                                  name
inaccessible
     firing
            winged
               edge
                  ahead the fiat
                         sphere
                         exhale
                              the
                                  expiration
                                  resonance

as of my origins
          the apricot by the hazel
                      smoothed
                      smothered
marrow
seed-expelled
            from parallel hole
                        I was amazed
sounding box
              in
              clepsydra
              vortex
                        of aphasia
                     on saying
                              either

anche tu bruco filisteo

    filodossia

        d'ogni

        vaneggiamento

zagara

    fragra

o naufraga

      d'arancia

      ara

      arancione

        ione

         e

          il

           vuoto

solco freme più del pieno

essenza

    anima

      palma

      alma della mia mano

          non possesso

po-ematica

    linfa

    d'informe

      in

        stringhe

          auroranti

l'immenso diss-odo

    dira-dando

        siconio

        con siringhe al

          ringhio

d'iniqu-i-nters-tizi

      caini

      caimani da cronacario

ossi

you too philistine
        philodoxic maggot
                        of every
                        frenzied
tawny
        fragranced
or shipwrecked
                orange's
                ochre
                altar
                        ion
                        and
                                the
                                empty
ridge shudders more than full
essence
                animating
                        palm
                        soul of my hand
                                        not possessing
poetic-haematic
                        lymph
                of the unshaped
                                in
                                        aurorant
                                                syringes
crumbling the immense
dispelling
                syconium
                        with syringes
                                growling at
iniquitous - interstices
                        cainish
                        cronacarian caimans
        bones

dati
    alle fauci
        d'enfisemi
            emissari
                misirizzi
inerte riflesso
      di
        frinire
        sfinimento
           o cela l'eco
              acefala
                foce
apoplettica
aposio-pesi
      e misure
        mille
        armille
           illecebra
              alluci
                in
                  azione
l'opponibile pollice verso al
      polline
        inerziale
           indice
          d'indicibile
          in
             mignolo
               d'inezia
tirannica
  annod-a-ffanna
        d'abbaio
           abbaglio
              avanzi
            d'avanzi

torn
          from the jaws
                    of puppet
                              emissary
                              emphysemas
inert reflection
                    of
                         whining
                         weariness
                                   or hiding the echo
                                             headless
                                                       estuary
apoplectic
aposiopesis
                    and measures
                         myriads
                         armillae
                              flattering
                                   toes
                                        in
                                             action
    the opposable thumb down against
                    pollinating
                              inert
                              index
                         of unspeakable
                              to
                                   struggling
                         tiny
                              tyrannical
finger
          barking
                    dazzling
                              remains of
                              remains

anzi giunge

unge

d'afono

aforisma

risma tale

talché mezze

tacche

lappatori

lacché

del sopire

x

n

assale lassa

sonn-o-lenza

all'abbocco

abaco

branca

branco

brancola

aleatorio galleggia

mucido

già

allora

giallore latebroso

ipso facto

in

postumo

umore

imposta

adipe tepida

pidgin

ginepraio

carovana

vana vorace

fossil-eterno

reaches rather

oiling

aphonic

aphorism

such a ream

of low brow

louts

lapping

lackeys

lulling

perennial

assailing lax

somnolence

to catch

abacus

limb

shoal

writhes

aleatory mould

floats

already

lurking yellow

ipso facto

in

posthumous

humor

imposing

tepid fat

pidgin

brambles

caravan

vain voracious

eternal-fossil

già
al
lume
giallume

global

elminto miasma

asm-a-dombr-a-mbrosia

sennò

senno

senso

sonno

desolante

grugno

sommo

criticume

menno

men

sogna

assedi-o-mertoso

e

se

gessi

essi esigui cumani sillabi

guitti

ambigui

usurpa-tori

invacchire

da seta il baco

crisi

crisalide

sottratto

il

dato

sericeo

crisantemo

already
lights
yellow alum
global
wormy miasmas
asthma-inducing-ambrosia
else
sensible
sense
somnolent
desolating
clotted
snooty
snot-criticism
evirated
dreamless
dreams
subservient siege

even
if
casts
they expound cuman syllables
ambiguous
quips
bullshitting
mad-cowing
the worm with silk
crisis
chrysalis
deprived
of
silken
datum
chrysanthemum

                        d'assiomatico

                                     esizio

entropion

      non introspezione

              né osmotico spasmo

in pectore

ignavia

    viavai

         perpetrante pattume

                      piattume

eclettico

ecliss-i-mmane

             raglia

         sferraglia

              tsunami sulla guancia

del presente

    esente

       entelechia

schiaffo di Posidone

parassitario

        ossesso

        esso

        so

         omo

          o minimo

        nesso

       omesso

        messo

             addì

             addirsi

             addietro

             additivi

of axiomatic

entropic

decay

neither introspection

nor osmotic spasm

in pectore

listlessness

shilly-shally

perpetrating drossy

doldrums

eclectic

eclipse emanating

jarring

hubbub

tsunami on the cheek

of the present

exempting

code

blow to Poseidon

passasitic

obsessed

I know

less than man

least

nexus

omissis

located

dated

able

abject

additives

immutable

bitumen

immutabili

bitumi

t'orbi

non

turbi

dissi

p

inabissi

pro die

pro capite

profilo

dilania

procell-a-mnesica

lacera

la

cera

la cera persa

proficuo

profuso

ora

rio

dimentica

ansa

ta-l-ento

fluir

e

acqua squarcia

fulcro

cromatico

il

guizzo

ozio

di palindromico salmone

argine denigra

petulante

blinding

un

disturbing

dissipating

sinking

pro die

pro capite

profile

dissects

amnesic storm

lacerates

the

wax

the lost wax

proficuous

profusion

now

river

forgets

bed

talent

flows

water rips

chromatic

fulcrum

the

idle

flash

of palindrome salmon

overflows denigrating

petulant

chameleonic muttering

balbuzie camaleontica

palinsesto

schermo innalza

    elzeviro

      eviro-aferetico

          o

            eretico

              etico sudore

morde la terra

      t'erra rondine

          x l'acino

dall'indistinto al racemo

perfino avversi

    a versi

        sillabe smisurate

                indelebi-li-bellule

senza elitra

      a difesa

        esala iride

          ride radiante

             o

          radente

            x

          dente

opaco capo

      era lume o emulare

l-eta

  argo

    occhiuto

        estorto

        stormire

           forse

              s'ogni

                 are

                 areté

schematic
screen raised
      elzevir
   ·   evirating-apheresis
           or
             heretical
               ethical sweat
bites the earth
       errant swift
          seed-seeking
by instinct to the bunch
though adverse
    to verse
        clumsy syllables
             indelible firefly
wingless
    defending
       exhales rainbow
         radiant laughter
              or
        close
        loser
opaque head
      lighting or emulating

deadly lethari-c-argo
    eyed
      extorted
      storming
        perhaps
          of all
            altars
              areté
or collar
    wreck

o coll-are

    arenare

        era

      nera risacca

          a seppellire

                non

                    una

         risata

             fatidica

né

    selva oscura

il

poi

sopprime

      il prima e sale sparge

        ma

       prima o poi

            lesto più d'istante

universo

altri

  in filigrana

      anatema

          meta

         anal

          idiolatrica

separa tara pes-i

        punti

        cardinali

          inalienabil

            li

              non

                mero

                  contenitore

                  controcampo

guscio in

era
dark underflow
burying
not
one
fatal
laugh
nor
dark wood
to
then
choke
the first and scatter salt
but
sooner or later
in a blink
universe
others
in filigree
anathema
anal
end
idolatry
separates tare weight
cardinal
inalienable
points
no
mere
containing
counter field
hull in
hall
in
flux

uscio
    in
       flussi
     influssi alogici
              migrando
parola
       con l'ala m'ari
            il cuore
              quando t'archi
constellanti frammenti
di
  vette
divelte
       d-onde
       d'urgenza
              d'oltremare palpebre
                       brevi
schiuma
schiud-e-sclama
       amalgama
               dilemma
               dilegua
               dilav-a-rcana
                 lavagna

incerti confini
          in bali-a-ttardi
            t'ardi fiaccola
nell'usurai-a-rsura
            alien-a-neliti
                 radici
                 i
pass-i-mplosi
           silente inesplorato
                 ivi comprendo

a-logical influences
                    migrating
word
          winging harrows my
                              heart
                              when bowing
constellating fragments
of
tops
toppled
          by waves
          of urgency
                    by brief
                              overseas eyelids
foam
disclosing cooling
                    amalgamation
                              dilemma
                              dissolves
                              discoloring arcane
                                   slate
uncertain confines
          intrepid-daring
          late- lights the beacon
in usury- drought
                alien-yearning
                        roots
the step-imploded
                silent unexplored
                                   where I grasp
the
non
passive sounds
                    unexpected
                         taut

i
non
passivi suoni
                inattesi
                    tesi
                antitesi
                    in voce
                tess-i-ridescenza
                                        eppur
nonostante
                minuziosamente
radar
    daranno
    da
        ranno annunciata perdita
                                    s'evince
amena
            proliferato tare filo
                                orpello
amente
        e
amen
        o
            lume
                già
                    mento
                        e volto
                                oltre
                                    sembianza

antithesis

in rainbow-weave

voice

else

despite

fastidious

radar

proclaim

claiming

foreseeable announced loss

presuming

pleasant

proliferated surfeit thread

ornamental

fool

and

so be it

o

lumen

already

jowl

and turned face

beyond

countenance

42. Prelogica la Visione induce

Prelogica la Visione induce

                              la
                              coscienza
                              a comprendere
preludendo la ragione

                         Questo m'ispira la Dea Madre
seduta sul trono

                    severa

                    se

                         vera la vita oltre

                                        il
                                        reale
                    s'eleva
                    dall'animalità originaria nel partorire
                                                  la
                                                  Specie
Urge

        emerge al di là della nicchia d'insediamento l'origine comune
        e non solo del patrimonio genetico

                                   giacché l'umano è soprattutto
un anima-le culturale sull'impervio sentiero della civilizzazione che
non coincide minimamente con

                                        il
                                        mero
                                        progresso
Essenza l'immagine

                         e nude dune

                                   hortus conclusus
                                        espelle
                                        all'esperire
                                                  da
                                                  alla

Pre-logical the Vision induces

Pre-logical the Vision induces
                              the
                              consciousness
                              to comprehend
prelude to reason
                    This Mother Goddess inspires me
seated on her throne
stern
if
life beyond
                    the
                    real
rises true
from the original animality in delivering
                              the
                              Species
Urges
    Emerges beyond the niche of the seat of common origin
    not only of our genetic heritage
                              as the human is
                              above all
cultural soul-animal on the steep path of civilisation which
in no way coincides with
                         mere
                         progress
Essence, the image
                    and bare dunes
                              hortus conclusus
expels
                         on experience
                              bringing
        to

                                                  luce
e senza somiglianza
leso
l'esistere
              incarna e osa
                    oltre ogni grazia
                              s'erge
                                    mistero
                                    istero
d'ignita
dignità epifania
                    specular-mente
                              sorge
                                    d'istante dedalica
                                          estensione
radic-a-lare
              che losco
              non oscura
                          né ottus-o-ttunde
        Solo
        sospeso nell'abisso
                          sinaptico fulcro
                                    pupillare
                                compenetrazione
nascendo
        con
              battiti
        combatti
                    con
                        certo
                    sconcerto
                          all'Essere
                                    fluendo
Est-etica o
pat-etica

light
likenessless
lesioned
life
                    incarnates and defies
                        beyond all grace
                                        rises
                                                    hysteric
                                                    mystery
of ignited
   dignified epiphany
                            mirror-wise
                                    springs
                                        extension of
                                                Dedalic instance
radical-winged
                    that muddy
                    not obscure
                            nor obtuse obtunder
Solitary
            suspended in the abyss
                                        synaptic fulcrum
                                            reciprocal penetration of
                                                    pupils
born
   throbbing
                you strive

                with a
                    certain
                        bewilderment
                            towards Being
                                        flowing
Aesthetic or
pathetic

etichetta
Esca la parola dell'idea o

                     dall'idea

             la parola

         esca
Nella fisica

          le teorie o modelli sono approssimazioni
applicabili per un certo campo di fenomeni

                       fuori del quale
bisogna trovarne altri
consapevoli dei limiti intrinseci ma nonostante portatori
d'ulteriori progressi
D'altronde ogni descrizione deve affrontare
le limitazioni
proprie del linguaggio ordinario
 Mappare

                     appare non

                     è

Il saggio orientale

              non si preoccupa di spiegare le cose
ma di Vedere

          d'ottenere un'esperienza diretta dell'unità delle cose
Il Fare dell'artista
faro inducente è

         al

         Vedere

            s-ogni segno il-limita

                   non

               imita
smentendo l'assioma platonico

              e i tanti

              aitanti prematuri

                 antiprecoci rigurgiti
icastici
 castighi d'epigoni

etiquette
             Let the word issue from the idea or
                              from the idea
                the word
                                issue
In physics
                theories or models are but approximations
applicable to certain phenomenal fields
                                        outside of which
others need to be found
aware of the intrinsic limits and yet bearers
of further progress
                        Besides, every description must face
the limitations
inherent to ordinary language

The oriental sage
                    cares not to explain things
but to See
                    to glean direct experience of the unity of things
The artist's Doing
is to be
            Beacon Inducing to
                    See
                        whether every limitless seer-sign
                                        Imitates
belying the Platonic axiom
                            and the many
                            powerful premature
                                confident anti-precocious
                                        regurgitations

icastic
chastening epigones of

d'epigoni spacciatori dell'attuale

                        per

                        nuovo

Eppure

    chi non si perde

        non

           si

              trova

                    minatore dell'indistinto

                         indi

                            istinto

                                lampante

dell'invedibile

dell'invisibile

dell'indicibile

   indice

            c-osmo-si

                 pensi-eri

                 colpe-voli

                       le

                        ali

                           sgomento e stupore

   ölmek

   olmak

          l'implosione dell'Artista si verifica

        nell'esplosione dell'Opera

                        che non è la meta

né il parto l'arrivo

ma il principio

           cioè la Soglia

                  affaccio alla Visione

Dice Borges

          lo scrittore non esiste

               esiste la scrittura

epigones pawning off the topical

as

new

And yet

those who fail to lose themselves

fail

to

discover themselves

miners of the indistinct

whence

instinct flash of

indiscernible
invisible
indescribable
conjures

cosm-os-mosis

thought-full

guilt- flown

wings

bafflement and stupor

ölmek
olmak

the implosion of the Artist occurs

in the explosion of the Opus

which is not the goal

nor birth the destination

but the beginning

that is the Threshold

verge of the Vision

Borges says

the writer does not exist

writing exists

e Flaubert

Madame Bovary sono io

ecco
l'Autore

la Dea Madre

l'autoritratto

allarme
all'Armonia

l'Art-E'

Memoria del Futuro.

Domingo Notaro
(Museo delle Civiltà Anatoliche
Ankara-primavera 2004)

and Flaubert
   Madam Bovary is me

       behold
       the Author
the Mother Goddess
    the self-portrait

alarm
at Harmony
    Art IS
     Recollection of the Future.

       Domingo Notaro
      (Museum of Anatolian Civilisation
      Ankara-spring 2004)

43. Libero d'esser

Libero d'esser
libero
          nessun
          né
                    ovvio
                    avvio
                         violenza
                         lenz-a-ll-ama
                                        amalgama
                                             gamma irradia
                                        sgama
                         amigdala primeva
                                                  evanescenza
                                                       scelta
                                                       scepsi
                                                               sia
LIBERO
               alius et idem
                              medi
                         te
                              su
                                   ila-re-alità
appena pania
          panicità solcante
                              dissoda
                              dira-da
                                   da
                              nudando
                                        o imbui
                              andazzo
glaciale piressìa
concentrici

Free to be

Free to be
free
       no-one
       nor
              obvious
                     violent
              rev-up
              bait-on-hook
                            amalgamating
                                   gamma irradiates
                                   conjectures
                     primeval amygdale
                            evanescence
                                   chosen
                                   skepsis
                                          be
FREE
       alius et idem
                     means
                     you
                            bent on
                                   winging- hila-r-eality
hardly hazard
       harrowing panicism
                            shatters
                            scuttles
                                   from
                            baring
                                   or imbibing
                            drift
       concentric
       glacial pyrexia

cerchi
  chi
     gogna
     agogna
         roghi
        arroghi
              seppur virtuali
                         endemici
C-OSM-O-SI
       sinaptico
       sinfoniale
           il percepir
                 induzion-e
d'oscuro
  Sculto
      tale
      talea
      talento germinale
               non
       lento specchio
            o d'enturag-e-ntr-act
      alef
        d'alfa
           ad omega
      alerta
      aleggi
       giostri fuso
            con
              torsione affina
attimo x volta
        celeste
         estenua cellofan
           fantoccio
offusca
  scaduta sembianza

encircles
    those
    pleading
    pillories
        advocating
        arson
            though virtual
                endemic
      synaptic
      symphonic
C-OSM-O-SIS
        perception
           induction of
obscure
  I Sculpt
  such
  scions
      germinal genius
            no
        dim mirror of
           entourag-e-ntre-act
      aleph
        alpha
          to omega
      wakeful
      winging
      whirling coil
         with one
             torsion per
instant refining
      celestial vault
      attenuating cellophane
           puppet
obfuscating
  expired semblance

            sedato il
            dato
                prodromo
                     mord'orpello
                prodigo
                      infrang-i-nibente
                proda
                   fatale sclerosi
                          in
                   fetale
crisalide
         bozzolo
       abbozzo
             fulmineo
             splash
                 asfittico
                   oro domo
                       o
pomodoro semifero
pomo
         esplode
         implode
            larv-a-vra
                 agguato in mutazione
                          nel
                      trarne
nutrimento
         o dispersione
                 spreme
                   meningi
                     ingiunge
spleen
splendor-e-sprime
inducente pomo primevo
            evoca

                    sedated the
            given
                        prodrome
                                    mordaci-ornament
                        prodigious
                                    infrang-i-nhibiting
                        shore
                                    fatal sclerosis
                                                in
                                    foetal
chrysalis
                cocoon
                coaxes
                        fulminous
                                smothered
                            splash
                                    supple gold
                                            or
golden seminiferous
globe
            explodes
            implodes
                        larv-a-having
                                mutating ambush
                                            to
                                            sap
nourishment
                or despair
                            squeeze
                                meninges
                            compelling
spleen
splendour-expresses
inducing primeval globe
                evokes

vocabolo
bolo
ab origine
impervio
poi pervasi
scomunicanti
d'empireo
emporio d'ometteri
omertosi -stema
timico tumore
eclissi
clessidra
ardi
il perpetrare
d'incerta cenere
incetta
incessante
qual
l'amo
orale dell'afa
vola
allor
alloro soltanto
in
culinaria
mero proto
torpore
rebus esuber-ale
aleatorio
rio
o
riolite
con
ferma
azione

vocabular
bole
ab origine
impervious
then   pervaded
excommunicators
of empyrean
emporium of excluding
conniving–system
thymus tumor
eclipses
clepsydra
igniting
perpetration
of uncertain ash
incessantly
in-catches
as
the torrid
oral hook
flies
when
laurel
in culinary only
mere proto
torpor
all-edged rebus of
aleatory
a-validity
or
riolyte
with
firm
action
fleshes and bone-defies

incarna e osa

antitanatica

tana

utopico utero

intensa-mente

ingremba

l'ulteriore

foro
form-a-vverante
 orma

d'emerso

dall'opaco
dall'inerte guscio

uscio

co-scienza

con

passione

con

cavo suo

no silente

pneuma compenetrante

non d'Arte

mappare
m'appieno distanza

azzardosa

d'azzurro

constelli fragrando
da bulbo

già

cinto d'assedio

dismisura plasmante

preludiale
perd'io
per
   dire

antitatanatic

den

utopic uterus

intense-wise

en-wombs

ulterior

perforating

form- be-falling

foot-print

emerged

from the opaque

from the inert case

access

science -awake

with

passion

with

empty sound

no silent

compenetrating pneum

not of Art

to map

I fill-full hazardous

distance with

azure

constellating fragranting

from bulbs

already

besieged

moulding dis-measure

preluding by god

I lose

to

say

di
    selvosa pece
        pupillar est-etica
d'inedito
    impronta
      o
      onta
        tarma
         ancor-a-rsi
            d'arcano
            canoa
             o
deserti
  erti coaguli
      d'ematici papaveri
            ingorgan grano
d'usurai-a-rsura
poiché
    il
    poco
    ammonta
      o
      forse
      avvall-a-sfittico
        asfalto
          o
        altore
           d'amorfo
          amor
             folgorante
follia il
  lieve non allevi
      Memoria
        aire
      membrana

sylvan rosin
                    pupilar east-ethic
of novel
            taint
                    on
            tarnished
            termite
                        branded
                                    of arcane
                                        canoe
                                            or
deserts
    sheer coagulates
                        of haematic poppies
                                    choking grain with
usurer-drought
because
            the
            little
            amounts
                        or
                        maybe
                        furrows -asphyxiated
                                    asphalt
                                            or
                                    feeder of
                                    fulminating
                                    formless
                                            love
folly by
    levity unrelieved
                        Memory
                        thrust
                        multidimensional
    membrane

multidimensionale

              assorb-e-spande

d'illuvie

    vie

    vi

      è

        li

          sta

        l' istante

        d-istante

            antesi

                  o saturo spazio

                              intermolecolare

qual d'acqua e

              vento

                  diss-e-rra

                        la mia mano

                        lampante

                        latenza

linfa

d'infinito palpitare

        particellare sciame

                    danzando configura

d'indivisibile

    visione

          soggetto

                non

          soggiace

              d'inaccessibil

                    orgasmo

                        sol

                          l'inizio

e

    stasi

        il sonno stenti

absorb-expands

wet road-
    ways
    where
        stands
     distant
     instant
      sprout
            or saturated intermolecular
     space
as of water and
         wind
           un-clasps
               my hand
               lustrous

            latent
lymph of
infinite palpitating
     particle swarm

           dancing conjures
from invisible
     vision
       un-subjected
        subject
           of inaccessible
               orgasm
                  solar only
the
beginning
and
    stasis
       slumber strives

        stiva
          va
        vomere
               stana
               oniric-a-ntimateria
     involge
     invola

             rem
             remota
             emozione d'imprevedibile
                      precoce
                      presente
d'archetipo il-limite
evocativo vita covo
        vortice ci trovo
                 d'archivio
                 siderale
algore
albore carnale
     argillare genesi
           all'oppio
          oppone
               apnòico
a vacua frenesia
       eresia
      sia baleno
         enosigeo
             teso
               oro
                 siconio
matrice duttile metallo
        allotrio
            mass-a-ssume
d'aneliti radi-canti

stows

tows

    strange vomer

        unearths

        oneiric a-matter

   enfolds

   en-flies

      r.e.m.

      remote

       emotion of unforeseeable

            precocious

            present

of archetype un-limit-ness

evocative life I brood

    unearthing swirl

      of sidereal

        archives

chilly

carnal day-break

clayey genesis

     to opium

     opposes

        apnoeic

to vacuous frenzy

    may heresy

      be enosigean

       bursting

         thrusting

     gold

       syconium

ductile metal matrix

    allotrious

      mass-a-ssume

antichi

precorrimenti

entità

entropica

a vitale relativa

meta-fora

stillicidio

indomita pietra qual

indole

indolente

ottenebra

inghiotte

intrico

amnestico

d'amnio

embrional interazione

forma-li risonanze

Universo

altri

non edenico recinto

me

te

ora

questa è la questione

qui

quiete

eternata

nata metamorfosante

gemma

apical-e-mana

Scultura

dal senso dell'energia

all'energia del

Senso

of radical-en-chanted
    ancient cravings
                forerunning
                  entity
                  entropic
to relative vital
            meta-poring
                tantalising
indomitable petrous as
indolent
incline
          obtenebrates
                ingesting
                intrigue
                  forgetful of
amniotic
embryo–inter-action
                form-al resonances
Universe
      other
          non-edenic compound
                    me
                  you
                      now
hence the question
here
hush
    never-ending
        natural meta-morphing
        apical –emanating
      gem
Sculpture
        from sense of energy
            to energy of
        Sense

44. L'Art-E'

L'Art-E'
                ogni definizione
                                appen-ombra
mero assedio
                edenico recinto
                                intollerante
                                        anteporre
già
    astronauta d'un grembo
                                ognun
                                        d'altronde
la
creazione
                oltre
                        l'orizzonte della conoscenza
appunto
                non c'è
                        evoluzione
                                ma
                                        ulteriore
                                                sorgenza
posterior l'idea
                alla visione
                        e nessun concetto
può
sostituire il fare
                faro
                        Memoria del Futuro [1]
percepire
perciò
        pire inducenti
                        déstino
                        destìno

Art IS

Art IS
            every definition
                        barely-penumbra
mere siege
            intolerant
                        paradisiacal boundary

already
pre-poses
    each womb-astronaut
                besides

creation
            beyond
                        the horizon of knowledge
 in fact
        there is no
                    evolution
                            but
                                ulterior
                                        rising
the idea posterior
                to vision
                        and no concept
can
replace deed
            beacon
                    Memory of the Future[1]
perceive
            let inducing
pyres thus
            stir
                    fate

noesi

sia   nodale nudità

l'insito
supporto
sconvolgendo

vuoto

il

nucleo

l'involucro

dell'opera

d'inedito inoltrando
catastrofe

e

catarsi
  arsi
      i sedimenti
          dimentichi d'eroso frantumi
    arenosi
          in
    arenaria
          o d'emerso granito

assoluto

vertice

assolato

d'opposti remoti

lì

sta
l'istante
      ante rem
      antesi constellante
lì
l'invedibil

altrimenti o

altri

mentiranno

noesis
nodal nudity
innate
support
subverting
the void
nuclear
sheath
of the unique
work
emanating
catastrophes
and
catharsis
smouldering the
sediments
forgetful of
eroded
sandy
shards
in
sandstone
or protruding granite   absolute
sunny
summit
of remote opposites
there
stands
the   instant
ante rem
starry anthesis
there
unseeable
otherwise
others

di
   proto
      torpido
         esigui
           guitti
              invano
               vanno
                annoverando
                         ricettatori
d'inezie
   inerziale marasm-a-sfittico
         marcioso mercimonio
                   la-c-era
incerto nettare
         nell'incessante
                 feccia
                    o
invisibile
in
   visibilio
         dall'energia della materia
               alla materia
         dell'energia
            assurge
            urge
            è
lo stile
  ostile ad ogni maniera
             acme virtuosismo
                 ismo
                    non
c-osm-o-si
      vischioso ammuschire
                d'amorfo
speculare simmetria

                    will lie
about
     proto
     pointless
               sluggish
          upstarts
           vainly
           vaunting
                         receptacles
of trifles
     inert asphyxiating-mire
          stinking sell-out
                    ripping
uncertain nectar
          in the ceaseless
                    slush
                         or

invisible
blissfully
               from the energy of matter
                    to the matter
               of energy
                    arise
               the urge is

style
  hostile to all manner
                    virtuoso acme
                         ism
                                   not
c-osm-os- is
          viscous mossing
                    of amorphous
mirror-image symmetry

tra-sparenza presente

sparizione

apparenza

esuefazione

non

stupefazione

immagini

d'immagini

iniquie scorie iconiche

icastico

castigo

tra

scende assale

l'autenticità

non

cita

n'è

eccitata

cecità

il punto di vista

punto

paradosso

dossier fatale

quale rimozione

l'Artista

non ha contemporanei

un calpestio di stelle nelle vene

la

mente

inabissando

il concavo in convessa

fulmineo

rubente melograno

grano

ogni palpito

trans-parent present
disappearance
appearance
assuefaction
not
stupefaction
images
of images
iniquitous iconic waste
icastic
chastisement
trans
-scends assaults
authenticity
un-
citing
is
excited
blindness
the point of view
point
paradox
fatal dossier
as removal
the Artist
has no contemporaries
a stampede of stars in the veins
the
mind
sinking
the concave into convex
lightning-quick
pomegranate thieving
a grain
each throb

         non

sfera

celeste

perfetta levigata

    atavica parola

      a l'ora presente

Itaca

  da

  impervia

  proiezione

    e tr-Art-e

      crisi

       in

      crisalide

        azzardo

         ardo

          do

non giudico

  dico

    guardati dal

    guardare

      se t'impedisce

di

 Vedere

". . . solo a livello macroscopico il tempo
va sempre dal passato al futuro. . . ."

        R. Feynman

Domingo Notaro così afferma dell'Arte
già dai primi anni sessanta
    DNA

                                        not
perfectly polished
celestial
sphere
            atavic word
                        to present hour
Ithaca
        of
        impervious
            projection
                and mid-Art and
                        crisis
                            in
                        chrysalis
                            daring
                            ardent
                                I give
I do not judge
        but say
                beware of
                looking
                lest it prevent you
from
Seeing.

"…only at the macroscopic level does time proceed from past to
future…."

                        R. Feynman

Domingo Notaro spoke this way about art
as far back as the early nineteen seventies.
                        DNA

45. Compenetrazione pieno-vuoto

Compenetrazione pieno-vuoto
        vuoi tu
           utero
              st-ele-mentale
                d-arsi
                dirsi
sublime alla luce dare
          D'albero
           albe viscer-ali speculari
              le
              parti
              appartengono al reale
              il
              tutto
alla Visione
        Pluridimensionale co-scienz-a-urora
                e l'amor aromal è
alegiar impulsa
      pulsa del profondo
          ondosa danza
             free-mente carnale materia
L'inerzia intrinseca non è
          tenue condensa impercepibil
             erosa
             rosa
             osa
              sa la cruna
asol-a-ssolata
        passione
      dissipazione
          eterno l'attimo evidenzia o dissolve
Dissi-d-io

Plenty-full-void compenetration

Plenty-full-void compenetration
                        you yearn
                                uterus
                                        elemental stele
                                                burn-bestowing
                                                        deeming yourself
sublime in light giving
                        Of tree
                                dawns specular visceral -wings
                                                                the
                                                                parts
                                                        belong to the real
                                                The
                                                whole to
dawn-aware-awaking Pluridimensional Vision
                                                        love is aromal
winging impulse
                        pulse-beat of the deep
                                        wave-weaving dance
                                                trem-u-lous carnal matter
Intrinsic inertia is not
                                tenuous imperceptible condensation
                                                        eroded
                                                        rose
                                                        risks
                                                                knowing
the needle-eye
eye-let sun filled
                        passion
                dissipation
                                the eternal instant highlights or dissolves
dis-cord I said

va

    acuita

vacuità

        palpito

           tormento tra-sparir l'opaco

Prim-o-rdi-ali

     i voli germogliando

          osmotici vo-lumi .

squarcia l'ombra

     brama

        plasmando inoltra l'inedito

           d'immerso

Fermentan mosti

     stimolando acini planetari

            siderali

           grappoli

galattiche vigne

    ignendo l'esistenza

        e

       si

         stenta in

          mondo di gregari

entropico grigiore

cristallizza senza trasparire

       eppu-r-uppe

         l'infamia

         linfa

          mia

         e d'altri soli

           solitari

diseredati

   dati

     in pasto all'incuri-a-ssoluta

         assolutoria

          condensazione

vacuity

   wants

      sharpening

         throb

           torment transpiring the opaque

Prim-or-dial wings

          flights sprouting osmotic light-volumes

rent the shadow

     craves

       moulding forwarding the unprecedented

             immersed

grape-musts ferment

     stimulating planetary berries

          sidereal

            clusters

galactic vineyards

      igniting existence

        and

         effortful

         endeavouring in

         the gregarious world of

entropic grayness

 crystallizes un-revealing

      and none-the-less bursts forth

        infamy

        my

        lymph

        and that of other solitary

            suns

disinherited

    fed

      to absolute neglect

      absolving

        condensation

        with reality

con

densa del reale

tetro aedo

ma oltre parvenza d'allucinato spettro

arcobalen-a-nela

svelando intatta espressività

e già il gesto

porta

soglia

sulle tracce dell'Opera preesistente

al suo stesso sorgere

nell'ar-dire michelangiolesco

esco

o non

esco

sconfinante

sconfitte

e folgorazioni

inoltranti

questa la

question-è

remoti

moti oltre

l'orizzonte dell'uno e del tutto l'intuizione

e

il

caso

condensazione

con

densa

azione sdensando stilistica

stilla

stellare in volumetrici rapporti

ortivo

vo soggetto

dense

grim aidos

but beyond semblance of hallucinated spectre-spectrum

rainbow-yearning

revealing intact expressiveness

the gesture already

leads

to the

threshold

tracing pre-existing Work-wake

to its very source

in Michelangelesque bold-saying

I come forth

or not

come forth

encroaching

downfalls

and fulminations

forwarding this

that the

question is

remote

motions beyond

the horizon of one and all intuition

and

chance

condensation

with

dense

action shunning stylistic

stellar i

drop in ortive volumetric

ratios

I am subject to

jet not

                                        getto non
                                    assoggetto
                                    all'oggetto
dissoluzione in
    soluzione
            nel segno folgorante
                        errante o
                    aberrante
                            il futuro tramanda
                                        trama
                            ama nel presente
confluire trascolorando
                        plasm-a-neliti avverando
Ognuno
    unico sulla faccia della Terra
                        eppur
                            ad ESSERE non basta
Chimera
chi
    meramente
            mente
chi
    sterminando le lucciole non può pur pretendere di
    spacciar cieli usurpati per magiche lanterne
In noi senno connessioni
                        i geni minime unità
                                    del
                                    biologico
                                    patrimonio
verticalità generazionale
                    il
                    Genio
                        port-a-ll'orizzontalità valicante
                                    dell'Idea
della stessa sostanza del sogno della Veglia

subjected
to object
dissolution in
solution
in dazzling sign
errant or
aberrant
the future bequeaths
plot-weave
loving the present
merging trans-coloring
mould-yearning true-becoming
Each one
unique on Earth
yet
to BE does not suffice
Chimera
whoever
merely
lies
whoever
exterminating fireflies cannot even claim
to pass off usurped skies usurped for magic lanterns
In us wise connections
minimum gene units
of
biological
patrimony
generational verticality
Genius
brings to the horizon
bounds
of the Idea
the very substance of the Vigil dream
distilling me

distillar mi
desti
    spasmodico
        dico
    spasmo
    nell'ardire
           il fare
           faro è

Civiltà o
  viltà
    assilla
     illusa
       chi depreda
         preda è devastante
           vastità d'esiguo sua miseria
Non osi l'ossessione
frequentar
     l'Arte
       sarebbe sconfitta già
         al sol preludio
           l'ossesso
              è
             degli
             angeli

alienati
non dell'Artista
     Se basso guardi
     come se il mondo in spalle tu portassi
     per far tremar il cielo
         basta
          sputar
           nell'acquitrino
          la
           qui
          trino

awakens

spasmodic

defined

spasm

in the boldness

of doing

beacon

of

Civilization or

cowardice

haunts

whoever deluded

preys a

prey to the devastating

vastness of his meanness

Let obsession dare not

frequent

Art

lest it be defeated already

upon its prelude

the obsessed

are

alienated by

angels

not by the Artist

If you look down

as if bearing the world on your shoulders

to make the sky shudder

it suffices

to spit

in the sewer

whose

present

trine

impetus

ardi

impeto

in

petto

insonne l'occhio all'anelito mancante

proteso

oltre la punta del tuo naso

forse vedi

immemori quanto inconsapevoli

voli

etereo

te

reo dedali dipanando

nume

eri allarme

all'Armonia

minotauro l'amorfo

veglia coscienza

fulminea

oscill-a-zione

illimita non

imita

lampa l'essenza

e senza

assenza

creando per Vedere

ere

ed

attimi

DNA
IN-FINITO
IN NUCE INDUCE

burning

in

breast

insomniac eye yearn-lacking

          outstretched

               beyond the tip of your

nose

you see perhaps

       forgotten and unaware

           ethereal

              flights

                  ash-guilty mazes

unravelling

divine

    you were alert

        to Harmony

           minotaur the amorphous

            waking fleeting consciousness

oscillating action

      limitless

  does not imitate the flash's

       essence

       without

       essence

         creating to See

                eras

                  and

                    moments

                     which

IN-FINITE

DNA

LEADS INTO KERNEL

46. Prim-o-rdi-ali

Prim-o-rdi-ali
       ora
           dici
              no
              non
      lirici
    deliri
      limbicco
      limbico
      limo
         l'abiltà
         labilità
             loffio lod-o -dierno
     li
    polifonico
         senso
         sennò
         senno anoressico
allarme
all'armonia
fulmineo lum-è
        cento miliardi
            ardi
              di
                rete
                   neuronal
                      e
Via Lattea costellando
quia
    segna-l-etica
        d'affranta
          fratta entropica

Primordial wing-weave

Primordial wing-weave
                now
                        you utter
                                non
                                        lyrical no's
                                deliria
                                        limbic
                                        alembic
                                        loam
                                feeble judge-mental
                fallible present- day
                audible laudable
                ability
there
        polyphonic
                                sense
                or else
                anorexic sensibility
alarming
harmony is
fulminous lumen
                myriad milliards of
                                ardent
                                        neuronal
                                                        meshes
                                and

Milky Way constellating
as
        signal-ethic
                        of fraught entropic
                                fragment

non
    mero
  numero
        permotore cifra
            anima quanto
so-g-getto
qual ignoro sorge
          lampant-e-mergenza
discordanza
in
  scordanza
        memorando
           iro proto torpori

spazialità
      alita
        talmente
          mente comprende
                 oltre
                     ogn'illusionistica
prospettiv-a-ttendibile
  specchio
      sol
        è
         l'abisso
         abisso impenetrabil
                   è
                     dello
  specchio lo
  specchio
      agire non eriga
           ingannevole meta
l'identico non
  identifica né

no
    mere
        numeral
            permotoring cipher
                animates
sub-ject
I ignore arises
            flash-clear emergenc-y
discordance
in
dis-recall
    recalling
           I water-feed proto torpors

spatial breadth
      breed-breathing
          mindful
          mind full
             beyond
                all delusive
perspective
    specular plausibility
             sole-sun
              the abyss is

    mirror of
    mirrors'
            impenetrable abyss

        acting not erecting
                deceptive destination

the identical does not
    identify nor does

identità

    sembianza non

   sema

    emana

      realtà intronata

        nata

        naturale [1]

        innatural

          è

           l'Arte

allerta

   non

   serve

   mercimonio

      d'occulti persuasori

            né

estetizzante cristallo

     stallo

       coagulo coerente

        coevo

        coibente grumo

d'immaginazione

 immagine aniconica

      non clone

        di

        lattice

        parvenza

né

del

fato

fatua

fattualità

   effigi-e-ffimera

      di formalistici

identity
        emanate
        semes but
        semblances
                        reality bewildered
                                in-natured
                                natural [1]
                                unnatural
                                                Art
is
alert
        does not
        serve the
                vested interests
                                of occult persuaders
                                                        or
aestheticizing crystal
                        stalling
                                coherent coagulation
                                coeval
                                cementing clot
        of the imagination
        an-iconic image
                                non clone
                                        of
                                        latex
                                        aspect
nor
of
fatuous
fate
factuality
                        fleeting figment
                of formalistic
                        accumulative blocks

                                    blocchi accumulativi
semmai
                semantici
                se
                    mantici d'ulterior ariosità
                                                    spiri
                                                    ispiri
                                                    spirale
d'irraggiunto
    irraggiante intuizione
di
        stilla
in
        stilla
                sedimenti
                    dimentichi
                                    concrezion-e-clissante
Procellaria
                    il
                    volo non teorizza
                    vola
                            o sfracella
                                        a
procellosa scogliera
i mezzi
                non
dimezzino l'idea
                                né
                    idea
                            sufficiente al fare
                                            far
                                                è
collassare nell'urgenza
ivi le radici del cuore nutrono

semantic perchance
      when the
           bellows of further
      windy airiness
                     spire
                    inspiring
                    spirals
of unreached
    radiant intuition
from
    droplet
to
    droplet
    depositing
        oblivious
              concret-ion-eclipse
Stormy petrel's
          fearless flight
             flies
                soars
            or smashes in
                to
stormy reefs
may the
    means not
demean the idea
          nor
      the idea
          sufficient to make
              making
                is
collapse into urgency
where the heart's roots nourish
              the mind's

                              la
                              mente

fola
follia
        fiata
        fiat
            dello strumento della
                                        ragione
                                        raggiungere [2]
d'ibrido
            odissea
                        incessante
                                    inflitta
li
    qui
        do
            l'avara stasi
                            il
                                limite
                                li
                                    mite
                                        o dannat-a-mbivalenza
perpetuarsi
            arsi
            si
                i frondami
                            ami germinazioni
ossimo-ri-mossi
                ossidiana
                        naturale squarcia
                                        arciere
                                        cieco
                                            vedendo

lament

fable
folly
    forceful
    fiat
        of the instrument of
            reason
            reaching[2]
endless
    hybrid
      odyssey
         inflicted
there
    here
      I pose
        stingy stasis
           the
             limit
           the
             mild

          or damn- able-ambivalence
perpetuating
    kindling
    kindlings
      to love germination
oxymoron re-moving
    naturally
obsidian rift
    the sightless
      archer

ciò

che

ignora

d'aporia

sporadica

spora

radica

icaria non

icastica

la metafora

fora

la

meta

nell' affaccio

emozione avverando
ablativa vitalba

inducente

inoltrarsi

si

segno

sugge

ustiona

spaziale spasmo

morforisonanza

som-a-ssume

struttura d'oscura materia

aire

retame

membranza

vuoto

interior avviene-sterno

vuoto

seeing
that
which
ignores
of dubious
sporadic
spore
radicating
icaric not
icastic
the metaphor
perforates
the
target
on appearing

emotion validating
ablative clematis
invoking
incursion into
such
signs
sucking
burning
morphoresonance
spatial spasm

som-a-ssuming
structure of obscure material
airy
meshy
membrance
void
interior ex-tern-becoming

frattanto
frattale
      fremente quintessenza
cronico
crono
   orco vorace
       di
        consunt-o-bumbra
            da
            terso
            crepuscolo
a livida feccia
     sinuosi suoni
         disse
          minati
           solchi
             in
prematura dispersione
   di
     sfingi
     sfinteri
     sfiniti
       in dedali
         li dadi d'omissione
incessante disfatta
      sorda
      s'orda
      scorda

        da futil-e-litume
          tumefatto
accumulo predone
     t-ardi
       che

void
    fleeting
    fractal
        trembling quintessence
chronic
crone
      ogre voracity for
            consume-d- arkening
                      from
                      terse
                      twilight
to livid dregs
      sinuous sounds
           utter
              mined
                ridges
                     in
premature
dispersion
    of
      sphinxes
      finished
      sphincters
        in mazes
            the die of omission
incessant defeat
    deaf
      flock
      forgets

      by futil-e-litume
          tumefied
accumulating prowler
        belated

mai

in polvere

vere infatuazioni

inerti treni

dei

deserti

lesto miraggio riflette

disperdendo

tepore stas-i-mpetr-a-lgore

crogiolo

olocausto intergalattico

d'attrito logorio

logos

in-finito

nitore

eros

o

eroso

or-dire

non calembour

caleidoscopica

distorsione

primordiale

e

là

i

dromi

geroglifici grumi

indizi

orme

d'enorme

trama stessa

stesse

e ricompone

burning

never

residues of

veritable

infatuations

inert trains

of the

deserts

reflect swift mirage

dispersing

static- petrified-rut warmth

crucible of

intergalactic

holocaust

by attrition worn-out

word

in-finite

pure

eros

or

eroded

leit-weave

no catch-phrase

kaleidoscopic

distortion

primordial

and

where

lay

landmarks

hieroglyphic clots

clues

pointers to

ponderous

plot itself

infinita

mente

e

norme

normalire

né

col

mare

colmare l'incolmabile

giada

già

fluendo

ugual

e distinto

istinto

o

stinto aduna

ad

una

ad

una clessidra

l'assolo colossal

particellare celarsi

arsi

si

i vigneti

vignor-io

chi non osa

sa

chi

intuisce

non esegue

self-stays
and recomposes
infinite
mind
and
norms
normalise

nor
with
sea
fill the unfillable
already
flowing
jade

even
and distinct
instinct
or
pale pairing
hour
by
hour glass
colossal solo
particellary concealment
ardent
so
the vines
wine
whoever fails to dare
knowing

prosegue
      s-ogni
          emozione
              pensiero
      segno
desti
destino
     est-etico
        fluire
           da perpetuo letargo
imposto
  posto non più
       supporto
        orto
        ortodosso
           o amniotica sacca

tale pagina
tela
   porta
    ortivo grembo
        in
        soglia
          oltre il concavo
            convesso
vortice ci trovi
né statico né dinamico
        nell'oscuro
lampante faro
    il
   fare

                        those who
                                        intuit
do not carry out
        carry on
                    whole-dream
                            emotion
                                    thought
                        sign
                        stir
destiny
            est-ethic
                    flow
                            from perpetual lethargy
imposed
    posed no longer
                        supporting
                            orthodox
                            hortus
                            or amniotic sac

page like
 canvass
            hortive womb
            ushers
            threshold
                        beyond the concave
                                    convex
vortex you find us
neither static nor dynamic
                            in the obscure
beaming beacon
            the

d'inenarrabil

è grappolo

l'Evento

palindromo

il

viaggio

ritorno

rito

orno

no

dì

venir

verific-a-zzerando [3]

dove

e

d'esse non più

qual d'astro lume [4]

visceri

ali

in

fluire

configurante

[1] Darwin osserva

nell'ambito naturale

il

più

adatto

sopravvive

2

Dovere della scienza dimostrare

3

Non tutto s'evolve

vedi i batteri che esistono da tre

making
        of the ineffable
                    is cluster
                        the Event
palindrome
        the
            voyage
                rite
                return
                    I ornate
                    nay
                    day
                    advent
                        verifi -re-setting[3]
where
and
whence no longer
            lingers astral lumen[4]
gut
        wings
            in
                configurating

                flow

2

Darwin observes
            in the natural habitat
                        the
                        best
                        adapted
                        survive

3

The duty of science to demonstrate

4

miliardi
    di anni e più non sappiamo

5

    Non la stella ma il lume vediamo
                    il
                    SEGNO
d'anacronistici
      misticismi
            miser-a-ppare ogni divinazione
                                in

confronto

alle
    fondamentali equazioni della relatività generale
                della meccanica quantistica
   rispettivamente di
          Einstein e Derac
               alla decodifica del

        DNA

Not all evolves
                See bacteria which have existed for three billion
        years we know nothing else

5

Not the star but the lumen we see
                                        the
                                SIGN
of anachronistic
                mysticisms
                        miser-able all divination
compared

to
        fundamental equations of general relativity
                                of quantum
mechanics
  respectively of
                Einstein and Derac
                                to the
decoding of DNA

47. Sul filo dilania (Angela)

Sul filo dilania
                    d'onirici
          diluvi
                l'esistenza
              e
                si
                    stenta
intimo
        rito
              immaginare
d'ardori
dardi
      in
          cipria
              d'onice
                        argine
                                denigra
                  sponda
                  risponda
d'esuberanza
              ansa
dissolve
      alveo perpetuo
                    o forse varca
                        va
                        arca
stipa
stiva
      affastella
            stellari
                  d-istanti pupille
in

On the thread-edge (Angela)

On the thread-edge sundering

                              the existence
                              of oneiric

            deluges

                  and

                        endeavouring to

imagine

            intimate

                  ritual

of ardour-ardent
darts

            in

                  onyx

                        powder

                              denigrates
                              staunching
                              shore
                              retort

of
exuberance
            the inlet
dissolving

                  perpetual bed

                        or even crossing

                              cross-over

                                    ark

hoards
hold

      stores

            stellar

                  pupil-instances

where

infiniti
    tini
        ivi fermenti
                molecole
                    colei
di
grani
turbini
    in me nascente spiga

non
d'indistinto grumo ammasso
                  assomma
                      ma
                        altro
tu
    naufraga
        fragando
                d'immerso
lapillare
gemmea pula
            aria dispersa
carnai
    alabastro
        astro
        astrolabio d'incombusta
                      gioia
lieto accogli
litorale segreto
            resinosa
              osa urgenza
ora
   alita
oralità
      ritorno

    in
      vast
      vats
        she ferments
          molecules
of
seed wisps
whirlwinding
         in me nascent sprout
not
of indistinct coagulated sum
           summing
              but
                other
you
    shipwreck
      wrecking
         of immersed
lapillary
gemmed air-scattered
        chaff
charnel houses
      alabaster
       aster
       astrolabe of non-combusted
              joy
joyfully welcoming
secret resinous
       littoral
         daring urgency
now

    breathes
orality
      returning

non

rito

orno

sonoro

ma

tralci avvita

vita

della tua vigna

ignito

di

grappoli

impastami

fremente

mente

te

tepore

orezza

azzera

ossido

d'oblio

d'ombra muffa vanifica

vinifica

di

vino

libar

mi

millibar anima

nidifica

nella mia mano

azzurrandomi

germi

in

ali

lampi

s-ogni

                    no
                rite
                ornating
                            sonorous
                                    but
weaving
            vital
                    trellis of
                            your vineyard
                                    bright
with
clusters
smear me
            quivering
                    mind
                        you
                            shadow-fall -annulling
                            warmth
oxide

            of oblivion
            the shade of mould vanifies
                                winifies
of
        wine
                pour
                        me
                        millibar soul
nesting
in my hand
                        azuring m
germs
            in-haling
                wings
                        every-dream

vegli-a-ccende
calancami
cavalla
cava
all'emozionale linfa
svelante
tenerezza
indagami
indaco
d'indicibile sonno
risacca
accaso
ora
amaranto
amar
mar
uv-a-urorale
soffio
fiorendo
e
brezza
nel
fluire

flashes
    watch-vigil-light

ravine me
she-steed
quarry-steep
    till emotional sap
        revealing
           tenderness
searching
sapphire
    of unutterable sleep
        undertow
          I wed

now
    amaranth
     marine
    amor
    aurora-grape
       breath-puff
       brushing

and
       breeze
          in
           flowing

48. Dall'irraggiunto irraggi percezione

Dall'irraggiunto
    irraggi
        percezione
            perduta-mente
                avvinta
non loquace
    loquela
        agape
    appaga
        affranto
          frantoio
             h
              d
                esistenza
                    olo-baco-vocabolo
                      evoca
plas-mare
plasma
      luminosa onda
            con-creta-mente
                incarna
fulgido
fulcro
    divora
        nutre
          e-l-avrà-larvale
              vale
                buco nero
e-loppar-trappole
      trapela
        la nudità del seme
            che

From the unreached let perception radiate

From the unreached let
        perception
            radiate
                lost-mind-less
                        captivated
non-loquacious
    loquacity
          sates
          satisfies
                grief-stricken
                grinder
                    h
                    d
                      existence
                        holo-bug-vocab
                          evokes
sea-patterning
plasma
        bright wave
              with-concrete-mind
                          incarnates
fulgid
fulcrum
      devours
          feeds
              larval-elevating
                worth
                    black hole
trap-enveloping
    leaks
        the nudity of seed
              that

sfarina

e

impasto

li-è-vita

prim-o-rdi

albedo

il

bandolo

penetrale

sfatare

sfavilla

fulminea d'opaco emana

o

dopando

le

norme

l'enorme

sul

filo

dilania

matassa

assorda-ladr-o-ssa

argine

argentei

annichilire

d'ere

esiguo

guado

erbe-ne-tenebre

brev-i-ntridono

comuni-

canti

antica

aporia

evapori

crumbles

and

dough

life-leaven

prime-val

albedo

the

penetrating

skein-end

myth-exploding

swift

spark of opaque emanates

or

doping

the

norms

the enormous

on the

edge

slaying

coil

dross-deafening

silvery

shore

to annihilate

of eras

the exiguous

ford

herbal-darkness

short-seeping

common-communal

chants

ancient

aporias

evaporate

e-pure-rupe

d'inezia

inizia

inerzia

inesorabil

sol

solca

caporalesco accalappio

messianico

marpione

traversie

traveste

in

festa

infesta

a chi non cela danna

e

linfa

infama

aduna

duna

rena

annott-a-rdesia

d'ogni smarrimento

sfalda

arsi

asettico

malor-a-ccumula

vili

trofei

miserrime

vittorie

reconditi profitti

smisurati

pure reef too
                    of inexorable
                        smidgen
                        starting
                        sloth
                                    sole
                                    sign

menial messianic
                    grovel-grabbing
                                    thieving thug
                                                travesty
                                                trick-clothed
in
festive attire
    infesting
                    damning whoever fails to hide
                                            and
                                            sap
                                            slanders
                                            assembles
                                            sand
                                                    dune
be-nighting slate
                    of all bewilderment
                                            crumbles
                                                burnt
aseptic
            mal-accumulating
                            vile
                            trophies
                                    wretched
                                    victories
inestimable
                hidden profits

di

fetidi

profeti

feticci

manna

mannara

cancrena pervasiva

lage-r-egala

relitti

relativ-a-vania

anima

anile

predone

predominio

osò-mu-fumoso

bove

boria

boiale

tal ismo capì

perpetuo inghippo

blatero

blatte

fin

anzi

brumosi

increspan

espanden

in

te

atro

atroce

spettrale chi ottunde

insueto

iscienza

scempio

of
fetid
prophets
fetishes
werewolf
manna
pervasive gangrene lager-donating

flotsam
taxing relative
animus
anile
predator
predominance
dare-mu-smoky
stupid
slaying
ism-grasping
smugness
perpetual pitfall
chattering
cockroaches
even
contrary to
cloudy
crinkle
expanding
in
you
spooky
spectral
shadow-grim
blunting
un-common
- sense mayhem of

d'arsenico minuzia

  arse

    nitore

      invesca

        vile

       vesco

         a

           mercenaria

           mercé

              di

           mèrce

              assidua

              assiderare

proscenio

    ai-global-e-la-bolgia

         dubbi

            o

         ubbie

           perplesso

             so

ilare

  e-liba-l-abile

      balenio

        lesta s'invola

          la

           in

            fondo

già-ce vertiginosa vetta

       per

        chi

         comprende

           oltre

ogni capienza della mano

       approdo

        dolente

arsenic minutia
    burning
        clarity
           luring
             vile
           devouring at the
                  mercenary
                  mercy
                    of
                  merchandise
                      assiduous
                      assideration
proscenium
        to-global hell-pit
              fears
                  or
             fancies
                puzzled
                  I know
hilarious
        blame-less-able
             glint
              deftly darts
                  there behind
                  after
                  all

already-there vertiginous summit lies
        for whoever
           comprehends
             beyond
all the hand can hold
        havening
           hurtful
           fraud

dolo

conclusorto

    o

       punt- o-rti-vo

           esterrefatta

            attanaglia

immortalità

    alita

immota

    sa

      di

        cristallo

          e-rapito-ti-pare

             ribalta

               la

             ribalta

espugna

 spugna

    altrimenti

      mentitori frettolosi

         da

          lurida latrina

caligine

calando

    esile coltre

        òbici

       d'obesi abissi

          ancòi

           colpita

l'ulteriore guancia

      o

        educare

        carenze

         si

          remote

hortus conclusus

      or

         ortive point

            amazed

              gripping

immortality

      breathes

motionless

     knowing

       of

        crystal

        enraptured-thinking

             oversetting

               the front

             of stage

expunges

 sponge

     otherwise

       fleeting fibbers

          by

           lurid latrine

haze

decreasing

     thin blanket

        obices

       of obese abysses

           today

             struck the

other cheek

    or

     educate

       shortcomings

         so

          remote

            with

                                        di
                                    certezza
                                    incertezza

diluire
diluvi
di
    galattica lava
            avari l'andare lordando
dilemma
    lemma
        mai
            dilegua
                    se-te

                    se

                        me
                    emerso dissetando albori
a-te-o-Poeta
                da
                    fissile parola
                                enucleare
                                            o
                    fossil
                        è
                        mucillagine
                                    senza
                                        confine
eco-nomi-a
                antisostanza
                            grigio
                                giogo
                                    al
                            gioco
                                    fecondo
                                        dell'immenso
accumulato dal caos

  certainty

                                        uncertainty

diluting

floods

of

        galactic lava

        greed-going soiling

dilemma

  lemma

        never

          slaking

               thirst

                    if

                  I seed

                        merged thirst-sating dawn

to-you-oh-Poet

              by

                  fissile word

                        enucleating

                              or

                  fossil

                is

                     mucilage

                        without

                        border

economy

      ant-substance

              gray

                yoke

                 to

              the play of the

                     fecundity of

                          immensity

accumulated from chaos

            chance finds

il caso trova

e solo a difesa

chiuso

il

pugno

o ustoria

storia senza fine

né principi

indicibil

il

dire

e-di-gru-turgide

idee

ali

cosmico crogiuolo

energia gron-dare

d'indistinto

intorpidito

ostaggio

aggioga

nel metallo

mantice

ammanti

spiegato

sulfureo avvampa

prisco

presagire

di

prismi

incute

incudine

qual gemmea melagrana

gravità

insita

vita

                              and only in defence
the   closed
fist
            or warp-wave
                    never ending story
                                    nor principles
                          unspeakable
                              to
                          speak of
an -crane-turgid
                    ideas
                          wings of
                                    cosmic crucible
energy-drip-giving
                          by indistinct
                              benumbed
                                    hostage
                                        yokes
in metal
            bellows
      mantling
                  unfolding
                        sulphurous blaze
                                    primary
presage
              of
                  prisms
                        strikes
                        anvil
                        as gemming pomegranate
severity
              inherent
      life
        dance
                  peak-nestling dynamic

danza

    a-cima-nida dinamica

          nudità

           per

            va

             si

            va

          inaudita

bolle di spazio

    acina

    coscienza

      anzi

        mai

         vuoto

      ansima

        quantico campo

dischiud-e-nigma

     osso-darà-paradosso

         oscura

energia

   repulsivo serraglio

       o

       oblo

       d'oblio

     erra

      l'io

        verba volant

galattici filamenti

     ma-te-ri-a-ppare

        dal

letargo

  argonauta

    anni

     chi

      l'ire

nudity

goes

per-

vading

unheard-of

space bubbles

seedling

consciousness

rather

never

void

panting

quantum field

enigma-dis-closing

bone-giving-paradox

dark

energy

repulsive menagerie

or

porthole of

forgetfulness

roam-erring

the ego

verba volant

galactic filaments

matter-you-appear

from

hibernation

argonaut

years

whoever

ire

returns

floating

riporta

fluttuante

endogeno

emergendo

d-istante

istantanea

stana

stanotte

3

P

Dante

d'albore

indovarsi *

* *L'imago al cerchio e come vi s'indova*   *Dante*

chi

luce vede nell'ombra

o

chi

adombra

ogni

lume

sulla cresta dell' onta

o

ontico

preludi

ali le messi

sinuose

fecond-a-ura trascolora

plasmando

gene-si

irradia

endogenous

emerging

of distant-instant

instantaneous

expels

tonight eager

3

P

Dante

of dawn

conformed *

* the Image to the circle conformed, Dante

whoever

sees light in shadow

or

whoever

shades

each

light

on the crest of dishonor

or

ontic

preludes

sinuous

wing-crops

fecundity trans-colors

shaping

gene-genesis

radiates

alienates yearning in

aliena-nei-la

la forma

anelito-ti-lena

arcobalena

postero

in

canto

infiamma

aria

attra-versi

icari

a

prosaica

sparizione

ossesso

o

onnivoro

la sfida

a

tale

sfinge

la

finzion-è

evo

evochi d'avi

radic-i-ridati

d'ignoto

sema

emana

la

lacrima solca

fulcro

fulge

gemico volto

vuoto

forms

strong–yearning

chant-enchanted

rainbow

heir

inflaming

air

through

icaric verse

to

prosaic

disappearance

obsessed

or

omnivorous

challenge

to

certain

sphinx

remote

forebear evoking

figment

of iridescent roots

of

unknown

emblem-

emanating

the

tear-track

fire

fulcrum

empty

gem-effigy

of earth's

erratic likeness

della terra
    erratico ritratto
        esule
          o
            naufrago
fossil mai
    vestigia
      già
    vesti
      il
        real-è-storta ragione
reticolati
    lati
      tanti
        d'opaco
         opachi
           della bilancia lago
              ossidi
seppi
    procura
      d'occaso lacerti
           a
            diniego

exile

or

cast-away

fossil never

vestige

already

dressing in

real-distorted reason

netted

sides of

many

opaque

opaque-nesses

lake balance

oxides

I knew

mandate

of lacerated sun-setting

to

denial

49. "Amor fia grave il memorar presente"

"Amor fia grave il memorar presente"

Cominciamento
        mentovar dei flussi
                iride
                    palpito e foglio
                    palpo
                    al
                        poi
                            spaziando
preludial
      albore
          tumide labbra
          tu
            mi
              dai
                  siconio a nutrimento
                            nitida soglia
                 sinfoniale
                    estesa
                        spoglia
                          liscia
                          scia d'impronunciato
impronta
      in
          disperdenza
                  contrappunto
                        dissonantemerge
se vuoi volare
            apice
           cela inizio
                tuo

"Love will render present recollection grave"

"Love will render present recollection grave"

The start of
    recollecting fluxes
                    iris
                    pulse and paper
                    palpating
                                to the
                                then
                                        broad-sweeping
preludial
        dawn
            turgid lips
        you
                offer
                    me
                    syconium to nourish
                                        limpid symphonic
                    edge
                    extended
                                simple
                                    smooth
                                    wake of
unspoken footprint
            in
            fade-out
                        counterpoint
                                        dissonance-merge
if you yearn to fly
                apex
                    conceals the start of
                            your

                         orlo dissolto
                                   traguardi
o
   vedi
        li
        linfaffonda
                  onda
                  da
                       sedimenti
                          dimentichi elementi
                                 e
                             le
                                menti perdersi
                                   per
                                       dirsi
                                          eretici
                                               s-ogni
sema
semmai
          somatico
          sonar del desio
                          antro
                          antropico
                                cavea
                                caverna
                                      golfo
                                          anfiteatro
amor assola
        assoluto
             utopia
                  o amara
                  amarra
                          fra-di-cio
                               avvers-a-vvera
rifrange

dissolve-edged
goals
or
see
there
lymph-drowned
wave
of
sediments
forget items
and
the
mind-elements self-lose you
to
be klept
heretics
of-each

sign
if anything,
somatic
sonar desire
anthropic
cave
cavea
cavern

gulf

amphitheater

love sun-lighting
absolute
utopia
or bitter
berth-rope
sodden
adverse event

tra
   mare
tra
   monti
tramuti
     in
       chi
         ostro
           alla notte sfuggendo
                 endogeno
                   enorme
                    orme
                    ormai
sa
sanguestorto
      iper-bari-che
          i-muti-bitumi
             misteri-che
deviate
   a-te-roma
      per-fida
         che
           tu
             sia
               incessante grinfie
                  infierir le
sorti
sortilegi
   egida dei foschi
      foschia
        iaculo
          cul de sac
             nel marasma
              asmatica
               atimia

refracts
  amid
    sea
  amid
    mountains
  changing
      in
        whoever
          night escaping
            west-wind
                  endogenous
                    gigantic
                        tracks now
                        traces
knowing
blood-extorted
          hyper-baric
                  dumb-bitumen
                      mysteries-that
diverted you
    atheroma-Rome
          faith-less
            you
                are
                  both
                      relentless clutches
                          cruel-inflicting
feckless
fate
    aegis of dark
          drizzle
              jaculus
                  cul de sac
                      in asthmatic
                        marasmus

                                        miasmatica
estetica
stitica
        mistificagognato in
                gogna
eticassente
                subdolo rebus
                                ubiquo
                                        o illuso
                                                rio dilacera
                                                        deriva
perturbando
                tanto inquietante
                                è
                        la
                                bellezza
                                        interazione
più
    dell'aria
            lieve
                e del sorriso
                                d-ante-l-io
                                        essenzialenergia
la sua grazia
                emanazion estrema
                                fremito
                                        alare
alabastro struggente
        astro
            d'allegria
                    al falò del tuo sguardo
                                ardor
                                    è
                                        o fragil-ita-li-a
qual

miasmatic

atimia

constipated

aesthetics

mystify-aspiring in

ethic-lacking

pillory

devious puzzle

ubiquitous

or deluded

river of lacerated

drift

perturbing

so disturbing

is

the

beauty of

interaction

more

than air

light

and of smile

of dante-ante-aura

energy essence

his grace

extreme emanation

wing-like

thrill

poignant alabaster

aster

of merriment

in the fire-glow of your eyes

ardour

either

fragility

qualità disattende
       stelo
         eloquente stilla
              qual
                 gemica vite
alla potatura istilla
       stillicidio
          umiliata
            anelito mancant-è
stagn-i-niquo
       ottunde

sipario
     demenza
         a-tale-celata
        talea
        talismanica
        tamagno
            inverosimil
               bluf
               blateraddobba
sudario
     sparto
      partenogenesi
      partenopea
         partiti
          i bastimenti
             permangono
orridimbrattando
        d'estorto
         orto
          tossicoblio
            liofobo
               coibentespoliazione
danna

as
quality disregarding
   stem
     eloquently distils
       what in
        gem-full vine
pruning instils
    drop-insisting
     humiliated
      yearn-lacking is
iniquitous slue
   blunts

curtain
   dementia
    hidden
    talismanic
    talea
    tamagno
      unlikely
        bluff
        blather-adorns
 esparto
   shroud
     Pathenopean
     parthenogenesis
      parties
       the ships
         remain
horror-besmirching
     of extorted
    hortus
      toxic oblivion
       lyophobic
        insulating sack

Napoli
   li
     immersa
     immensa vita
          denudando snodi
               di erose
                  rose germinali
in-cute
    pietre l-avi-che
          umano patrimonio
         patria
           stuprata
lo stesso cuore
      erompe ross-astro
           pulsar
             d'amorfo
             amor
              morfonema
               né
                 mai
prono
   ostico
    iconoclasta
        habeas corpus
           va
           vampa pensiero

                    odi
                    o
                     diversità
armonizzare
     sol
       lecita
       felicità
         o farmaco

damns
    Naples
        its
          immersed
          immense life
                baring joints
                         of eroded
                           germinating roses
in-stills
    ancient lava stones
             human heritage
                   raped
             homeland
the heart itself
          ross-starred erupts
                pulsar
                  of amorphous
                  amor
                   morphoneme
                     or
                        never
prone
    adamantine
      iconoclast
           habeas corpus
                 goes
                 blazing thought
                            ode-hear-hates
                            or
                             diversity
harmonizing
        licit
         soh-solo
        happiness

meco socratica cicuta
dell'uno
il molteplice
si
compie
giorno
non
orno
te
muto
tananài
tana
fanatica
foss-e-ss-o-ssimoro-rimosso
rarefazione
non
azione
faziosa
a
iosa
afasica coscienza
invaccaccumulo
ulteriore confino
inopinabile
bilharzia
infino
terso mondo solcando
argin
e
il
punto
d'incontro
controcampo
intuitivo
intrinseco svelando

or drug

with me Socratic hemlock

of the one

the manifold

is

attained

day

un-

adorned

you

mute

dinning

addicted

den

as if removed ox-y-moron

rarefaction

not

factious

action

ga-

lore

aphasic consciousness

cow-ing-cumulus

ulterior undisputable

confinement bilharzia

endless

cloudless world ploughing

dam

and

meeting

point

of intuitive

reverse shot

costellan

gli

occhi

al rossore

fulminee

galassie s'allontanan

sfiora respiro e

il cielo

della Terra

erra umica edera

ed

è

viva

argenteargilla

desti

destillar

s-ogn-i-ncompiuti

d'io bambino e

in

tanti adulti

intenti

sopravvissuti

intatti

soltanto

nelle

membra

dalla città premeva

premeva

atmosfera

agro

groviglio d'avverso

verso

linfa

ovunque insonne bulicame

impercettibile

intrinsic unveiling

           constellating

                the

                    eyes

                        to fleeting

                              redness

galaxies move apart

              breath-brushing and

                  the sky

of Earth

      err-wanders humic ivy

           and

           is

           live

             silver-sand

                    awakening

                    distilling

un-finished dreams

           of ego child and

                in

                  many adults

                surviving

                  intent

                  intact

                    only

                      in the

                        limbs

by city pressed

      pressed

           atmosphere

              sour

              tangle of adverse

                  verse-tending

                  sap

wherever sleepless bullicame

brina

fluttuando dileguar

qual

da

clessidra

irretita sabbia

così partimmo

lesi

all'esistere legati

ingabbiati

gabbiani

dai

flutti

donde pre-terito

ritorno

minuscolo

scolaro

non

scoloro

d'atavico ulivo

discreto

intensità coltivo

conosco radiose

e derise stagioni

d'intemperie

giacinti

in giacimenti

intimi

trova melograna

dei

palpiti

plasma

chiude

schiude

tremi

                              faint
                              frost
fluctuating slipped away
                              like
                          from an
                                hourglass
                                        enmeshed sand
so we set out
                       injured
                    bound to existence
                                    gaoled
                                    gulls
                                         by
                                             wave-ebb-flow
hence preterit
                    return
                              miniature
                                 scholar
                                      I did not
                            discolor
                                     discreet ancestral
                                              olive
of cultivated intensity
                       I know radiant
                                   and derided seasons of
bad weather
                      hyacinths
                   in intimate
                      deposits
                              locating pomegranate
                                             of
                                          heartbeats
plasma
          closes
        discloses

        mirto immemorabile

             ogni dove

allora

    voltinfossati di stenti

         d'ignito

          ignoto nel ventre

vento

v-entrava

     d'eclissi

        rappreso dall'arsura

             che

              più

                del tempo

smisurato ingromma

       assale

       sale usura

         anomalo

         malore

           sapere

esponenzial-è

     a quanto ignoro

         precario lucore

             orezzare

nonostante

non

assorto alla

  sorte

    agli antipodi

       in piroscafi salpammo

            protési

a forgiare

    la

      fortuna

        oltreoceano

        oltre

                    trembling
                        immemorial myrtle
                                everywhere
then
        hollow-faced hardship
                        coal-digging
                            unknown in the belly
wind
there- entered
            of eclipse
                    returning drought
                                that
                                    more than
                                        boundless weather
en-grimes
                        assailing salt-wearing
                                anomalous
                                illness
                                        to know is
exponential
                as I fail to
                        inhale
                        precarious glow

although
not
absorbed in the
    fate
            poles apart
                    in steamers we sailed
                                    bent on
forging
            fortune
                there
                    overseas

ogni pròtesi

di
stasi
plumbeassilli
lampi
in
pasto
impasto
pervade d'indicibile
parole
germoglianti
ammali
appena
enarra
pulviscolar
scolarca
insito scalpitar
scolpita
mano
nel sapiente gesto
gestazion
è
o estolle-re-moto
congesto
gesticolio
ciarlierorigami
amidaceo
cerbero
a-cran-i-narca
a
un
filo
spinto speme
o

over

each prosthesis

of

lead-assailing

stasis

flashes
fed to
dough

pervading of unutterable

words

budding

sickening

as soon as

telling

dusty

scholarch

inherent clatter

carved

hand

in wise gesture

gestation

is

either up-ward motion

congested

gesticulation

chatty-origami

starchy

Cerberus

skull-raised

to

a

thread- edge

pressing hope

or

spino

    proteiforme

        orme d'esiguo

            guado

                ad rem

                    da tempra

                          del

                          metallo

                            allotropia

tempesta scarna

          e lo scarlatto in tenebra

                    ebra

                      freddandosi

possente

        impronta

           a dismisura

                      a-meta-patema

                      emana

                          alveo duplice

inghiott-e-rutta

        abisso

          issofatto

              impeto

              in

                petto

              o

            impetra

                eraclito divenire

recondito turbi-na

          d'Urbe

              e-se-qui-e

                  fiumesonda

cicatric-i-ncrudelite

        credulità

protean-form
     thorn
          small
               ford-trace
                    of relevant
                         tempering
                                   in
                                   metal
                                        allotropy
gaunt gale
               and I scarlet in tenebrous
                         stunned
                              cooling
mighty
          mark
               of disproportion

                         half-heartache
                              emanates
                                   two-fold bed
swallow-eruption
          abyss
          ipso facto
                    impetus
                    in
                         pectoris
                    or
               petrifying
                         Heraclitus becoming
recondite turbine
               of Urbe
               and-if-here-be
                         river-over-flow
scar be-cruelling
          credulity

sgomenta

      e d'avvenire il presente

alquanto

    manca

      e nello stesso due volte

          niuno si bagna

             o

l'ego

legò e

lega

   corpo-reo magma

      amniotico ingremba

         e

         dalle

         soglie

varcate

   non sempre vi è ritorno

       inauditi

        itinerari

in

  scissossario

     iner-te

     iner-me

     insito

     insidia tal egoismo

        indissolubil

mente

   versione

  perversione

  pervenuta

     ancor

  perdura

    di girare le pagine

       attonite dita

        avvertita

dismaying

of the future the present

somewhat

lacking

and twice in which

no one bathes twice over

or

the ego

alloyed

alloy

body-offending magma

amniotic en-wombing

is

from

verges

crossed

there is not always return

unheard

itineraries

in

bone-dividing

inert you

inert me

inherent

endanger this in dissoluble

selfishness

mind-lying

version

perversion

proceeding

still

persists

in turning pages

astonished fingers

aware of

l'urgenza
      tanta lenta l'attesa
           incerta ora
             origlia
             raglian
             gli
               abbagli
impantanan l'estro i miraggi
      le
        strade
        estranean
          ad ogni altrove
            ove
            verifica
era-bruto-turbare
        arenili perpetui
            dissolti brividi
              idiozia
or
  già
orgia
    ammutolit-e-mozioni
          i-divi-li-vidi
            carn-a-lita
alienare
     affranti
      antichi
     canti
       incanti
       incauti accanimenti dissimular
l'assenza
     furtivi
     furfanti
     fanti
     fantocci

urgency
   of long-slow uncertain
      wait now
        eavesdrops
        braying
        the
         blunder- glares
bogging down inspired mirages
    the
     roadways
    estranging
      at every elsewhere
       where
       it verifies
brute-era-troubling
     perpetual beaches
       dissolved chilling
        idiocy
or
 recent
 revel
  silenced emotions
     livid divine
      carnality
alienate
  distraught
   ancient
  chants
   incautious insistent incantations
   dissembling
absence
  furtive
  felons
  foot-soldiering-knavish
  finger-puppets

occidui

numi virili

viralilarilluni

afferrar

ferrami

ossid-a-zione cementizia

amianti-ca-ncrena

salute

assorta

d-an-nata

cannibalesca

esca

l-i-perbole

ipso facto

<u>qui-e</u>-*scienza*

il prossimo dissimil

e

ma

qui

al

quia

mero

facsimil

è

cupi

di

già

esule-deluse

e avulso dal sentire

tire

e

molla

chi

odo

schiaccia

declining
virile numi
viral-lari-luni
gripping
ferrous
oxide en-acting cement
asbestos-gangrene
health
absorbed by
yearly-born
cannibalistic
bait
the ipso facto
hyperbole

<u>here is</u> science-quietus
proximate dissimilating
and
though
here
because
mere
facsimile
is
deep-dark
with
already
exile-hope-dashed
detached from feeling
give
and
take
whoever
I hear
crunches

chi
  odo
     vaneggia
       già
         aroma-si-disamora
                barbuglii
                barbagli
                   gli
schizzi lascian
  la
    sciami
        sedimenti
         dimentichi fibrillazioni
               di
                frasi
                franan
                frantuman
tabù-la-rasa
        fossi
         li
          dispersi
             repente
             reperti
             reperire
                era-ludo-modulare
soli
  da
solitudine
    neppur cavalchi
        chi osceno
          scempio
      cavalcar
        ti
         vuole
          ergi-ti-gre

whoever
   I hear
      vain-raves
         already
            aroma-dis-in-amors
                    babbling
                    blind-flash
                      the

spray quits
    the
      swarms
         sediments
         forgetful fibrillations
                 of
                  phrases
                  falling
                  fragmenting

tabula rasa
      as if
         the
           dispersed
               sudden
               dig-finds
               dis-covering
                  ludo-modular-era

only
  from
solitude
    never riding
        not even those who obscene
                  besmirching
      straddle
        wanting
        you
          tiger-towering

                impervia

                   via

               ignavia

                       disattende

gelo-si

    del fuoco specular

             eccesso

            e cessò

               cespugli

                spogli

                   senti-eri

eppur

    radi

    radicar avvera

          tal passione

               nei grappoli autunnali

pigiatura

      e dei fermenti

          nuova

            linfa decanta

                 nonostante

pania

    anche il

pane

    test

      arda la mente

          d'inadeguato

            guado spalanca

                 inguaribil

nel cuore arcobalena

        tumultuosa

           fiumana

          emana metamorfica

              orfica

sillepsi o icaria

                              impervious
                                sloth
                                way
                                  disregarding
icy- jealous
        of specular fire
                        excess
                          ceased
                            bare
                            bushes
                              pathway-sense you were
yet
 sparse
      root come true
                  such passion
                            in autumn cluster-bunches
press
            and from ferments
                      new
                        lymph decants
                              despite
snare
      and also
bread
        stubborn
          burns the mind
                    of inadequate
                        ford throw open
                                  incurable
heart rainbow
                  tumultuous
                        flood
                          emanating metamorphic
                                    orphic
syllepsis or icaria

                    brucia
                         s'inoltra
                              m'allocco
                                   coll-uso costume
all'occasione
     occasi
          lievi
               tare dilania
                    amnesia sincope
                                        a
                                             dimora
i-se-mi-mesi
               imprenscindibil
                         era-d-ossi-diss-o-dare
cinestesia
          o bislacche fisime
                         di mene in
                         men
                              che non si dica
e lusinghe unico approdo
                    ingabbi
                         gabando
                              vamparsura
                                        al
aspro
     fondo
          i-puri-dirupi
               ustorio specchio
                                   di
                                   quali
                                   bramosie
d-onde spettro sonoro
                    senza requie
                         schiuma
                              mare

burns

entering

fooling me

conniving custom for

the occasion

obscuring

slight

tare slaying

amnesia syncope

to

house

the seed months

imperative

was-of-oxy-till-ing

kinaesthetic

or weird whims

of intrigues in

less than

no time at all

and lures sole landing-place

ensnaring

duping

flame-thirst

in

bitter

depths

the pure-crag

burning mirror

of

such

cravings

whence wave sound spectrum

restlessly

foams

sea

                         già

te

tersicorea

        colmare mai si colma

                  sciacquio vacilla

assale

scialbo

scialacquo

       omerico sbadiglio

               in

               corpo

                 rare

                   post rem

velluto tulle vela

         arché

         arcare

           serici piumaggi

               ossid-a-bisso

d-a-c-qui-trino

        nume

          immune grumo

            umor

              esco-rt

              escogitare

sosta

 ostare

      ad ogni proseguire

             ingordo

             gorgo propizio

                 per

                  durare

vessa postremo

         concentrici cerchi

             ma

            non

you
dancing
> never full fills

> > > lapping falter

storms
stolid
squandered
> Homeric yawn

> > in

> > body

> > > rare

> > > > post rem

velvet tulle sail
> arché
> en-arching

> > silky plumage

> > > oxides abyss

of present cesspool
> numen

> > immune congeal

> > humor

> > > escort

> > > contriving

pauses
precluding
> at each progression

> > greedy
> > eddy propitious

> > > to

> > > > en-during

vexing subsequent
> concentric circles

> > you do

> > not

                                    trovi
nonostante la visione
                        desti
                il palpitare
                                    timo
                                o
                                rosa
                                        con-chiglia
diss-e-rrando
                    molecolare spasmo
                                accresce
                                decresce
                                        pur
                                            infimo
                                            infinito
polisemia di consonant-i-mpregna
                                    e
                        vocal
                                    incantate
essenza
e senza torpore
            tarpare
                    aggiogant-i-nani
                                rudi-mentali
                                        a
longeva
            lungimiranza
                        l'oro
                            a
                                noi
                                noi
                            a
                    loro
                                tuttavia specchietti e croci
pungente l'aria

find

despite vision

the pulse of
thyme
or
rose-pink
shell with

unwound-wandering
molecular spasm
increases
decreases
even the
lowest
infinite

polysemy of consonant- impregnate
and
vocal-evoking
enchanted

essence
and numb-less
wing-clip
rude-mental
yoked-dwarfs
to

long-living
foresight
their gold
to
us
ours
to
them
however mirrors and crosses

piercing the air

                    e
                         lontana
        gente
             all'orizzonte
                              penetra pioggiarsura
                                        smeraldo
nardo
        spigo
                 inarrivabil
                      e
                    tra
                      sparire
                                ed esser
                                     ovunqu-è
il centro della sfera
                 spirale
                 aspira
                    e del profondo
                                tumulto
incombe terrestre
                 estrema
                      lacer-a-zione
                      la
                         c'era
                              d'avverso
                              a verso
                                   oltre la prosa
                                        prosaica
materia prima
                 a
             prima
materia
             d'enti
                 di natura
                      a

                    and
                        distant
        people
                on the horizon
                            penetrate dark-rain
                                            emerald
spikenard
    unreachable
            aspic
                    and
                        between
                            disappearing
                                and being
                                    wherever
    the centre of the sphere
                    spiral
                    aspiring
                        and profound
                                    tumult
    looms terrestrial
                    extreme
                            lacer-action
                            there
                                wax-was
                                    of adverse
                                        verse-tending
                                            over prose
                                                prosaic
    raw material
                    to
                    primeval
    matter
                of entities
                        of nature
                            to

denti di
dentiere
addentanti
inneschi feroci
basta
arda
ardesia
sia cadmio e
d'iridescenza indaco
indago
irrefrenabil penna
lapis
lapislazzuli
estremo firmamento
avvinto
persoscuro
scarabocchio
scardinante
ibrido
brivido
e-li-tu-n-i-nutile
oltre
il
sapere
ere-d-ere
erede
inaudito nobel all'inedito
o
sol
somiglianza
azzardo
ardo
do
portento
tento

teeth of
dentures
biting
terrible triggers
enough
burn-bastard
slate
both cadmium and
iridescent indigo
I investigate
un-brake-able pen
lapis lazuli lapis

extreme firmament
enthralled
dusk-lost
doodle
unhinging
hybrid
thrill
and use-less-you
over
the
knowledge
of inheriting
heir
unheard-of un-listened-to Nobel of innovative
or
simple
similarity
I dare to
hazard
attempting
portent
I try

almeno
    intercettare

P.S.
    e leste
      stelle
          stiano
              pure a guardare

at least

    to intercept

P.S.

    and may
   the deft-swift
        stars continue
       to look
          down

50. Intraducibilità della Poesia *A Kay McCarthy*

di
luce
propria
illumina
s'ognuno unico è
e irripetibil
è
forse ingenita
a
   tal
      originarietà
e
all'originalità
   alità
      alita
         insita
            oltreché
               meramente linguistica
oppur
appura
   pura immagine
      immagina
         tradurre
         indurr -è
            d-unica partitura
inscindibil
      forma-contenuto
qual
quarta dimensione
all' avverarsi
      nulla
        è più reale

The untranslatable nature of poetry *To Kay McCarthy*

of
its own
light
it shines
if each is unique
and ir-repeat-
able be
inborn maybe
to
    similar
            origin-root
and
to originality
        wingedness's

            breath
                    inherent
                            beyond
                                merely linguistic
or rather
ascertains
    pure image
        imagines
            translating
            inducing
                sole score's
indivis-ible
                content-form

    as
fourth dimension
of realisation

                    del
                      vero
e
  nulla
                 più
                  vero
                      della
                           vision-è
est-etica
          sinfonia
                    in
  nuova
  esecuzione

Dublino
                        estate 2013

nothing
is more real
than
truth
and
nothing
more
true
than
vision which is
ethical-aesthetic
symphony
in
new
rendition

Dublin
summer 2013

DOMINGO NOTARO
PAINTER, SCULPTOR, POET

1939 Born on December 27 in Palermiti, Calabria, Italy.

1949 He joins his family members in Argentina.

1958 He attends the Fine Arts Academy, Buenos Aires, where he holds his first personal exhibition.

1961 He invents *"chinacido"* (a combination of India ink and acids) which allows him to obtain explosive, throbbing, vivid colors.

1963 He returns to Italy. He lives two years in Florence before moving to Rome, where he still lives today.

1965 New York, *Guggenheim Museum*, his work is exhibited alongside works by Chagall, Dufy, Léger, Modigliani, Picasso.

Personal exhibitions, Publications, Conferences, Awards

1965 Rome, *Quantas Gallery*, presentation by David Alfaros Siqueiros.

1965 The work *"Crocifissione"* [Crucifixation] defined by Waldemar George as the most important work of art of the post-war period.

1966 A guest of Pablo Picasso's at Nôtre Dame de Vie. A great friendship is born.

1966 Rome, Galleria 88; Chieti.

1967 Paris. Two personal exhibitions, Louis Aragon, Jean Cassou, Waldemar George write about him.

1968–69 Bruxelles, Knokke, Porto Cervo, Viterbo, Salerno, Naples at the city's historic *Maschio Angioino* bastion.

1970 Zagabria, Belgrade, Dubrovnik, travelling retrospective of 223 works, hosted by the Academy of Arts and Science, Yugoslavia.

1971 Rome, the *La Nuova Pesa* gallery.

1972 Naples. He is conferred with the "Posillipo d'Oro per l'Arte" [Posillipo gold award for art].

1972 Turin, Alba, Alessandria: Pablo Picasso sends a telegram of esteem and friendship.

1973 Ferrara, *Palazzo deiDiamanti*, a retrospect of 133 works.

1973 Rome, *Silarte Gallery*, presented by Giorgio Bassani.

1976 Sorrento, the Torquato Tasso institute publishes *I miei piedi sono radici d'aria* [*My feet are roots of air*], a collection of poems.

1977 Catanzaro, Provincial Hall, retrospect.

1981 Frascati, Town Hall, exhibition care of the CNR scientific community.

1982–88 Todi, Soverato and Velletri, exhibition in collaboration with the Enrico Fermi Institute.

1990 Rome, the San Michele a Ripa Monumental Complex, retrospect 1960-1990.

1991 Tokyo, Metropolitan Art Space, retrospect 1960-1990.

1995 Rome, Casa Argentina.

1995 Tucumàn, MuseoTimoteo Navarro and Fine Arts Academy.

1996 Sovera ed. publishes *D'èsili esili che questo tempo impone* [*Of exile exiles these times impose*], with a preface by Walter Pedullà.

1999 An essay by the author on "Arte e Poesia" ["Art and Poetry"] in *Come nasce l'opera d'arte* [*How a work of art is born*], published by Edizioni ELDEC.

2000 "*OLTRE L'ORIZZONTE*" ["Beyond the Horizon"], homage to Domingo Notaro. Paintings, drawings, sculptures, poetry. ELDEC publishing house, Rome.

2001 Rome. The Vittoriano monumental complex, "*Oltre l'Orizzonte*" ["Beyond the Horizon"],1960-2001 retrospect.

2003 Palermiti, Honorary citizenship.

2003 Rome, Capitol Hill, Town Hall, the *Brutium* Gold Medal

2004 Istanbul, *Ilayda* gallery.

2004 Ankara, University of Bilkent's Art Gallery.

2005 Palermo, *Aula Bunker* at the city's tribunal, he composes "*Allarme all'ARMONIA*" ["Alarm to Harmony"] dedicated to Giovanni Falcone.

2005 Ankara, the "Adnan Ötüken" Library, "*Lo sguardo di un'artista italiano sull'arte ad Ankara*" ["An artist's view of art in Ankara"].

2005 Ankara, "*Dall'Eufrate al Mediterraneo*" ["From the Euphrates to the Mediterranean"].Research of the Italian Archaeological Mission in Turkey. Composes the publication's cover and graphic design.

2005 Ankara, Cankaya Contemporary Arts Centre, "*Memoria del Futuro*" ["Memory of the Future"], a 1960 – 2006 retrospective exhibition.

2005 Ankara, Museum of Anatolian Civilization, "*Memoria del Futuro*" ["Memory of the Future"], a personal exhibition of works devoted to the culture of Anatolia, presented during the official visit of the then President of the Italian Republic, Carlo Azeglio Ciampi.

2006 Ankara. Creates the logo for the 150th anniversary of Italo-Turkish diplomatic relations.

2006 Ankara. Guest of the Middle Eastern Technical University, at the invitation of the Rector, Prof.Dr.Ural Akbulut.

2006 Ankara. Guest of honor at the Middle Eastern Technical University's 8th Arts Festival.

2006 Ankara, Middle Eastern Technical University, conference by Carlo Guaraldo, "Domingo Notaro: an artist scientist," to celebrate the Year of Physics.

2006–07 Ankara. Designs IN-NUCE INDUCE, cast later in bronze.

2006 Diyarbakır, KeciBurcu, personal exhibition of drawings dedicated to the civilizations of Anatolia.

2006 For the Middle Eastern Technical University Ankara, he sculpts *DNA* using Nano-technology.

2007 Ankara, for the Sihirli Bahçe Montessori School, "*Dall'indistinto lampa l'ART-È*" ["From the indistinct flash Art Is"], a single work (5m x 2m) starting from the schoolchildren's drawings.

2007 Ankara, *Ilayda* Gallery, personal exhibition.

2007 Ankara, METU, "*Oltre lo sguardo la Visione dell'Opera*" ["Beyond sight the vision of the work"] a single work (5m x 2m) starting from children's drawings.

2007 Ankara. Creates a logo for the Embassy of Italy to celebrate the "150th Anniversary of Italo-Turkish Diplomatic Relations."

2007 Ankara, METU, "*Turche-si Stagioni*," ["Turk-uoise seasons"] a personal exhibition with two sculptures and 80 pictorial works composed during his two years at the University.

2007 Ankara, the Prefect, Kemal Onal, presents the Artist with a testimony of merit.

2008 "Riviera dei Marmi," International Poetry Award, first prize.

2008 The President of the Republic, Giorgio Napolitano, makes him a Knight of the Order of the Star of Italian Solidarity.

2009 Ankara, he creates the logo for the European Kaleidoscope Europe-Cultural Bridges project.

2009 Ankara, he creates the logo for the 50th year of the Italian Institute of Culture.

2009 Rome, for the Italian Embassy in Ankara he creates the "*Italia in Turchia 2010*" ["Italy in Turkey 2010"] initiative's logo.

2009 North Cyprus, Middle Eastern Technical University, a series of art and painting workshops and meetings.

2010 Ankara, publication of the book of poetry *Libero d'esser* [*Free to be*], care of the Kanguru publishing house, presented at the International Book Fair, Istanbul.

2010 Rome, seat of the Friuli Venezia Giulia Region, Piazza Colonna.A personal exhibition with writings by Renzo Tondo, President of the Region, and Carlo Guaraldo, Director of Research, National Institute of Nuclear Physics.

2010 Rome, Rotary International. *District Governor's Citation* awarded to Domingo Notaro for his contribution on the occasion of the organization's 105th anniversary.

2010 Istanbul, *Galleri Daire 1*. Personal exhibition of works created in Turkey.

2010 Rome, the Italian Foreign Ministry, Palazzo della Farnesina. On November 16, a Ceremony of Donation to Italy of an anthological selection of one hundred works, following an exchange of letters with the President of the Republic, Giorgio Napolitano; presentation by art historian Vittorio Sgarbi, before the authorities and Carlo Marsili, former Ambassador of Italy to the Republic of Turkey.

On this occasion, Notaro is created a Knight of the Order of the Star of Italian Solidarity.

2011 Rome, *Ara Pacis* museum. Notaro participates in an exhibition promoted by the Foreign Ministry called "Il palazzo della Farnesina e le sue collezioni."

2011–12 Damascus, Italian Embassy, permanent exhibition of twenty works.

2011–12 Tunisia, Centre National d'Art Vivant. Rabat, Ecole National d'Architecture. Algeria, Palais de Rais-Baston 23. The "*Il palazzo della Farnesina e le sue collezioni*" traveling exhibition sponsored by the Ministry of Foreign Affairs within the ambit of which he represents Italian art with nineteen works.

2012 London, Italian Institute of Culture. Domingo Notaro takes part in an exhibition organized by the Ministry of Foreign Affairs called "*Il palazzo della Farnesina e le sue collezioni.*"

2013 Dublin, *Farmleigh Gallery*. Kaleidoscope, Contemporary Art from EU Members States. Exhibition organized by The Office of Public Works, Department of Arts, Heritage and Gaeltacht, Irish Presidency of the Council of the European Union. Domingo Notaro represents Italy with a selection of his works.

2015 Dublin, publication of the book of poetry *The mind elements of words* [*E-le-menti delle parole*], care of The Daedalus Press, with a preface by Catherine O'Brien, presented at *Trinity College Dublin*, *Long Room Hub* (Italian, English and Irish).

2016 Rome, at The *Yunus Emre* Turkish Institute of Culture, in Via Lancellotti, Rome, an exhibition of paintings and sculptures.

The following have written about Domingo Notaro:

Louis Aragon, Giorgio Bassani, Marziano Bernardi, Alberto Bevilacqua, Carlo Bo, Lorenzo Canova, Jean Cassou, Pierre Courtihion, Raymond Charmet, Augusto Gentili, Waldemar George, Kiymet Giray, Carlo Guaraldo, Vittorio Leti-Messina, Paolo Levi, Vittorio Mathieu, Aldo Passoni, Pavlov Pavlovich, Walter Pedullà, David Alfaros Siqueiros,

Leonardo Sciascia, Vittorio Sgarbi, Josip Skunca, Aydın Şimşek, Ken Waschin, Ümit Yasar Güzüm, Zeynep Yasa Yaman, and many more.

Enrica Maria Ferrara

Enrica Maria Ferrara (Ph.D., Reading, UK) lectures in Italian Studies at Trinity College Dublin and has published widely in the field of Italian and Comparative Literature. Among her most recent publications are a monograph on Italo Calvino and the theater (*Calvino e il teatro. Storia di una passione rimossa*, Peter Lang: Oxford, Bern, 2011) and a volume on the interaction between theatrical and narrative discourses in twentieth-century Italian literature (*Il realismo teatrale nella narrativa del Novecento: Vittorini, Pasolini, Calvino*, Firenze: Firenze University Press, 2014).

Kay McCarthy

Irish by birth, Italian by adoption, Kay McCarthy is a musician and aspirant polyglot. A graduate of the National University of Ireland, Galway, and Rome's Sapienza University, she is a language teacher and translator.

SELECTED DALKEY ARCHIVE TITLES

MICHAL AJVAZ, *The Golden Age.*
The Other City.
PIERRE ALBERT-BIROT, *Grabinoulor.*
YUZ ALESHKOVSKY, *Kangaroo.*
FELIPE ALFAU, *Chromos.*
Locos.
JOE AMATO, *Samuel Taylor's Last Night.*
IVAN ÂNGELO, *The Celebration.*
The Tower of Glass.
ANTÓNIO LOBO ANTUNES, *Knowledge of Hell.*
The Splendor of Portugal.
ALAIN ARIAS-MISSON, *Theatre of Incest.*
JOHN ASHBERY & JAMES SCHUYLER, *A Nest of Ninnies.*
ROBERT ASHLEY, *Perfect Lives.*
GABRIELA AVIGUR-ROTEM, *Heatwave and Crazy Birds.*
DJUNA BARNES, *Ladies Almanack.*
Ryder.
JOHN BARTH, *Letters.*
Sabbatical.
DONALD BARTHELME, *The King.*
Paradise.
SVETISLAV BASARA, *Chinese Letter.*
MIQUEL BAUÇÀ, *The Siege in the Room.*
RENÉ BELLETTO, *Dying.*
MAREK BIENCZYK, *Transparency.*
ANDREI BITOV, *Pushkin House.*
ANDREJ BLATNIK, *You Do Understand.*
Law of Desire.
LOUIS PAUL BOON, *Chapel Road.*
My Little War.
Summer in Termuren.
ROGER BOYLAN, *Killoyle.*
IGNÁCIO DE LOYOLA BRANDÃO, *Anonymous Celebrity.*
Zero.
BONNIE BREMSER, *Troia: Mexican Memoirs.*
CHRISTINE BROOKE-ROSE, *Amalgamemnon.*
BRIGID BROPHY, *In Transit.*
The Prancing Novelist.
GERALD L. BRUNS,

Modern Poetry and the Idea of Language.
GABRIELLE BURTON, *Heartbreak Hotel.*
MICHEL BUTOR, *Degrees.*
Mobile.
G. CABRERA INFANTE, *Infante's Inferno.*
Three Trapped Tigers.
JULIETA CAMPOS, *The Fear of Losing Eurydice.*
ANNE CARSON, *Eros the Bittersweet.*
ORLY CASTEL-BLOOM, *Dolly City.*
LOUIS-FERDINAND CÉLINE, *North.*
Conversations with Professor Y.
London Bridge.
MARIE CHAIX, *The Laurels of Lake Constance.*
HUGO CHARTERIS, *The Tide Is Right.*
ERIC CHEVILLARD, *Demolishing Nisard.*
The Author and Me.
MARC CHOLODENKO, *Mordechai Schamz.*
JOSHUA COHEN, *Witz.*
EMILY HOLMES COLEMAN, *The Shutter of Snow.*
ERIC CHEVILLARD, *The Author and Me.*
ROBERT COOVER, *A Night at the Movies.*
STANLEY CRAWFORD, *Log of the S.S. The Mrs Unguentine.*
Some Instructions to My Wife.
RENÉ CREVEL, *Putting My Foot in It.*
RALPH CUSACK, *Cadenza.*
NICHOLAS DELBANCO, *Sherbrookes.*
The Count of Concord.
NIGEL DENNIS, *Cards of Identity.*
PETER DIMOCK, *A Short Rhetoric for Leaving the Family.*
ARIEL DORFMAN, *Konfidenz.*
COLEMAN DOWELL, *Island People.*
Too Much Flesh and Jabez.
ARKADII DRAGOMOSHCHENKO, *Dust.*
RIKKI DUCORNET, *Phosphor in Dreamland.*
The Complete Butcher's Tales.

FOR A FULL LIST OF PUBLICATIONS, VISIT: www.dalkeyarchive.com

RIKKI DUCORNET (cont.), *The Jade Cabinet*.
The Fountains of Neptune.

WILLIAM EASTLAKE, *The Bamboo Bed*.
Castle Keep.
Lyric of the Circle Heart.

JEAN ECHENOZ, *Chopin's Move*.

STANLEY ELKIN, *A Bad Man*.
Criers and Kibitzers, Kibitzers and Criers.
The Dick Gibson Show.
The Franchiser.
The Living End.
Mrs. Ted Bliss.

FRANÇOIS EMMANUEL, *Invitation to a Voyage*.

PAUL EMOND, *The Dance of a Sham*.

SALVADOR ESPRIU, *Ariadne in the Grotesque Labyrinth*.

LESLIE A. FIEDLER, *Love and Death in the American Novel*.

JUAN FILLOY, *Op Oloop*.

ANDY FITCH, *Pop Poetics*.

GUSTAVE FLAUBERT, *Bouvard and Pécuchet*.

KASS FLEISHER, *Talking out of School*.

JON FOSSE, *Aliss at the Fire*.
Melancholy.

FORD MADOX FORD, *The March of Literature*.

MAX FRISCH, *I'm Not Stiller*.
Man in the Holocene.

CARLOS FUENTES, *Christopher Unborn*.
Distant Relations.
Terra Nostra.
Where the Air Is Clear.

TAKEHIKO FUKUNAGA, *Flowers of Grass*.

WILLIAM GADDIS, JR., *The Recognitions*.

JANICE GALLOWAY, *Foreign Parts*.
The Trick Is to Keep Breathing.

WILLIAM H. GASS, *Life Sentences*.
The Tunnel.
The World Within the Word.
Willie Masters' Lonesome Wife.

GÉRARD GAVARRY, *Hoppla! 1 2 3*.

ETIENNE GILSON, *The Arts of the Beautiful*.
Forms and Substances in the Arts.

C. S. GISCOMBE, *Giscome Road*.
Here.

DOUGLAS GLOVER, *Bad News of the Heart*.

WITOLD GOMBROWICZ, *A Kind of Testament*.

PAULO EMÍLIO SALES GOMES, *P's Three Women*.

GEORGI GOSPODINOV, *Natural Novel*.

JUAN GOYTISOLO, *Count Julian*.
Juan the Landless.
Makbara.
Marks of Identity.

HENRY GREEN, *Blindness*.
Concluding.
Doting.
Nothing.

JACK GREEN, *Fire the Bastards!*

JIŘÍ GRUŠA, *The Questionnaire*.

MELA HARTWIG, *Am I a Redundant Human Being?*

JOHN HAWKES, *The Passion Artist*.
Whistlejacket.

ELIZABETH HEIGHWAY, ED., *Contemporary Georgian Fiction*.

AIDAN HIGGINS, *Balcony of Europe*.
Blind Man's Bluff.
Bornholm Night-Ferry.
Langrishe, Go Down.
Scenes from a Receding Past.

KEIZO HINO, *Isle of Dreams*.

KAZUSHI HOSAKA, *Plainsong*.

ALDOUS HUXLEY, *Antic Hay*.
Point Counter Point.
Those Barren Leaves.
Time Must Have a Stop.

NAOYUKI II, *The Shadow of a Blue Cat*.

DRAGO JANČAR, *The Tree with No Name*.

MIKHEIL JAVAKHISHVILI, *Kvachi*.

GERT JONKE, *The Distant Sound*.
Homage to Czerny.
The System of Vienna.

FOR A FULL LIST OF PUBLICATIONS, VISIT: www.dalkeyarchive.com

JACQUES JOUET, *Mountain R.*
Savage.
Upstaged.
MIEKO KANAI, *The Word Book.*
YORAM KANIUK, *Life on Sandpaper.*
ZURAB KARUMIDZE, *Dagny.*
JOHN KELLY, *From Out of the City.*
HUGH KENNER, *Flaubert, Joyce*
and Beckett: The Stoic Comedians.
Joyce's Voices.
DANILO KIŠ, *The Attic.*
The Lute and the Scars.
Psalm 44.
A Tomb for Boris Davidovich.
ANITA KONKKA, *A Fool's Paradise.*
GEORGE KONRÁD, *The City Builder.*
TADEUSZ KONWICKI, *A Minor*
Apocalypse.
The Polish Complex.
ANNA KORDZAIA-SAMADASHVILI,
Me, Margarita.
MENIS KOUMANDAREAS, *Koula.*
ELAINE KRAF, *The Princess of 72nd Street.*
JIM KRUSOE, *Iceland.*
AYSE KULIN, *Farewell: A Mansion in*
Occupied Istanbul.
EMILIO LASCANO TEGUI, *On Elegance*
While Sleeping.
ERIC LAURRENT, *Do Not Touch.*
VIOLETTE LEDUC, *La Bâtarde.*
EDOUARD LEVÉ, *Autoportrait.*
Newspaper.
Suicide.
Works.
MARIO LEVI, *Istanbul Was a Fairy Tale.*
DEBORAH LEVY, *Billy and Girl.*
JOSÉ LEZAMA LIMA, *Paradiso.*
ROSA LIKSOM, *Dark Paradise.*
OSMAN LINS, *Avalovara.*
The Queen of the Prisons of Greece.
FLORIAN LIPUŠ, *The Errors of Young Tjaž.*
GORDON LISH, *Peru.*
ALF MACLOCHLAINN, *Out of Focus.*
Past Habitual.

The Corpus in the Library.
RON LOEWINSOHN, *Magnetic Field(s).*
YURI LOTMAN, *Non-Memoirs.*
D. KEITH MANO, *Take Five.*
MINA LOY, *Stories and Essays of Mina Loy.*
MICHELINE AHARONIAN MARCOM,
A Brief History of Yes.
The Mirror in the Well.
BEN MARCUS, *The Age of Wire and String.*
WALLACE MARKFIELD, *Teitlebaum's*
Window.
DAVID MARKSON, *Reader's Block.*
Wittgenstein's Mistress.
CAROLE MASO, *AVA.*
HISAKI MATSUURA, *Triangle.*
LADISLAV MATEJKA & KRYSTYNA
POMORSKA, EDS., *Readings in Russian*
Poetics: Formalist & Structuralist Views.
HARRY MATHEWS, *Cigarettes.*
The Conversions.
The Human Country.
The Journalist.
My Life in CIA.
Singular Pleasures.
The Sinking of the Odradek.
Stadium.
Tlooth.
HISAKI MATSUURA, *Triangle.*
DONAL MCLAUGHLIN, *beheading the*
virgin mary, and other stories.
JOSEPH MCELROY, *Night Soul and*
Other Stories.
ABDELWAHAB MEDDEB, *Talismano.*
GERHARD MEIER, *Isle of the Dead.*
HERMAN MELVILLE, *The Confidence-*
Man.
AMANDA MICHALOPOULOU, *I'd Like.*
STEVEN MILLHAUSER, *The Barnum*
Museum.
In the Penny Arcade.
RALPH J. MILLS, JR., *Essays on Poetry.*
MOMUS, *The Book of Jokes.*
CHRISTINE MONTALBETTI, *The Origin*
of Man.
Western.